PSI IN PSYCHOTHERAPY

Conventional and Nonconventional Healing of Mental Illness

PSI IN PSYCHOTHERAPY

Conventional and Nonconventional Healing of Mental Illness

by

ALEX TANOUS, D.D.
ELAINE SCHWINGE, M.D.
ANDREW F. BAMBRICK, PhD.

www.whitecrowbooks.com

Other available works by Alex Tanous:

Three Days of Darkness
Beyond Coincidence
Is Your Child Psychic?
Dreams, Symbols and Psychic Power
Conversations with Ghosts

For more information, visit the
Alex Tanous Foundation for Scientific Research
www.alextanous.org

PRAISE FOR
PSI IN PSYCHOTHERAPY
~

"This book is a rare treat showing us a glimpse into the future of psychotherapy through the visionary eyes of one of the most talented and academic psychics of the twentieth century. The unique collaboration between Alex Tanous and a marvellously open-minded psychiatrist offers a model for healing that transcends the current biopsychopharmacological paradigm. His ability to intuitively detect the roots of psychiatric illness in undisclosed childhood experiences and hidden ancestral influences and share them with clients in an illuminating fashion offers a foundation for research in clinical parapsychology."

~ Larry Burk, MD, CEHP, former board
president of the Rhine Research Center,
author of *Dreams that Can Save Your Life*
(Findhorn Press, 2018)

"A fascinating, moving and well-written account. Whether one believes in psychic phenomena as such or not, the study illustrates well how therapeutic techniques based upon such beliefs can be helpful and integrate with conventional therapy."

~ PROF FREDERICK TOATES, DPHIL, DSC, OPEN UNIVERSITY, AUTHOR OF *HOW SEXUAL DESIRE WORKS: THE ENIGMATIC URGE* (CAMBRIDGE UNIVERSITY PRESS, 2014)

"Every psychotherapist should be required to read this, and everyone having a psychic experience will gain insight from the book"

~ LOYD AUERBACH, MS, AUTHOR OF *PSYCHIC DREAMING* (LLEWELYN 2017)

"Old but new, this valuable work contributes to the emergence of the practical parapsychology of well-being. It also resonates with patterns previously underreported in the work of psychospiritually oriented healers both in and out of mainstream medicine and psychotherapy."

~ CHARLES F. EMMONS, PHD, GETTYSBURG COLLEGE, AUTHOR OF *CHINESE GHOSTS REVISITED* (BLACKSMITH BOOKS, 2017).

"This book suggests in choosing a suitable psycho-therapist, it is important of course to choose from the professionally qualified, but it may give a further vital advantage to choose someone with a true healing ability."

~ ANNEKATRIN PUHLE, PhD, AUTHOR OF
LIGHT CHANGES: EXPERIENCES IN THE PRESENCE
OF TRANSFORMING LIGHT
(WHITE CROW BOOKS, 2014)

"A fascinating book, dramatically hinting about the way psychic abilities may become practical tools for helping relieve suffering, although, on another level, even the thought of a psychic's connecting with another's mind can be rather frightening – for both real and irrational reasons."

~ CHARLES T. TART, PhD, AUTHOR OF *ALTERED*
STATES OF CONSCIOUSNESS
(HARPERCOLLINS, 1990)

"*Psi in Psychotherapy* presents a set of intriguing case studies arguing that talented psychics can provide valuable insights about clients engaged in psychotherapy. This book should be required reading for anyone interested in exploring enhanced techniques for treating mental health."

~ DEAN RADIN, PhD, CHIEF SCIENTIST, INSTITUTE OF NOETIC SCIENCES, AND AUTHOR OF *REAL MAGIC* (LISTENING LIBRARY, 2018)

"Dr. Tanous had his abilities tested on a number of occasions, and in this instance, turns them to the clinical setting. Empathy and intuition can go far in helping the client on the path to recovery."

~ ROSEMARIE PILKINGTON, PhD, EDITOR OF *MEN AND WOMEN OF PARAPSYCHOLOGY, PERSONAL REFLECTION*, 2 VOLS. (ANOMALIST BOOKS, 2013)

"When dealing with the concept of psi and the usage dealt with in this work it is of particular interest that the area of the practitioner or 'healer' and their attitudes towards the individual being treated/studied are so comprehensibly covered."

~ ROLAND ROTHERHAM, PhD, EdD, AUTHOR OF *SACRED FALLS* (ST NECTAN'S WATERFALL PUBLICATIONS, 2014)

"Though largely - as described in the foreword by Cooper and Krippner - 'a historical document', this book provides a fascinating and contemporary relevant account of the potential role of psychic diagnosis in psychotherapy. The original cases detailed date from the 1970s and 80s and are clearly of their time – nonetheless they provide currently relevant insight and understanding into how psychiatry and psychics might be brought together to develop therapeutically beneficial outcomes. At the original time of writing, Tanous and colleagues saw their work as 'a small step in the march for progress' towards a positive and collaborative future for psychics, psychotherapists and researchers. With the current growth in the field of parapsychology, Cooper and Krippner – in bringing this collection to a wider audience today – have made an additional large leap in the same direction."

~ SARA MACKIAN, PHD, OPEN UNIVERSITY,
AUTHOR OF *EVERYDAY SPIRITUALITY* (PALGRAVE
MACMILLAN, 2012)

"Alex Tanous was a genius at findings practical ways to apply his extensive skills to help people, and *Psi in Psychotherapy* is an example of one of his greatest efforts in this area. Many people who have psi experiences are looking for spiritual components to their psychological conditions, but very few professional counselors are familiar enough with the finding of parapsychology to provide an appropriate integrative diagnosis or plan of treatment."

~ JOHN G. KRUTH, MS, EXECUTIVE DIRECTOR,
RHINE RESEARCH CENTER.

An unconventional, bold and probably unique approach to the psychotherapeutic process, with a psychic and a psychiatrist both involved in the diagnosis and the healing. The psychic, Alex Tanous, attempts to identify clairvoyantly the clients' early experiences and their relationship to current problems, and his impressions are used in determining the treatment. The excellent introduction and afterword from eminent parapsychologists provide a clarifying context to evaluate this approach and understand it in today's terms. But it is the snippets of information about the healing of what appear to be incurable diseases, as well as his personality and beliefs, that make one want to find out more about this fascinating yet little-known figure.

~ ZOFIA WEAVER, PhD, AUTHOR OF *OTHER
REALITIES?: THE ENIGMA OF FRANEK KLUSKI'S
MEDIUMSHIP (WHITE CROW BOOKS 2015)*

CONTENTS

~

FOREWORD

~

This book has lain dormant for over three decades, until now, as it is brought into the light of publication. Like several manuscripts written by the late Dr. Alex Tanous, for reasons unknown to us, he never managed to see *Paranormal Psychotherapy* (as was its original title) to the point of publication. One can only assume time was not on his side when it came to the final editorial demands of the manuscripts, alongside his guest lecturing commitments worldwide. Tanous constantly wrote on a wide variety of topics within the realms of parapsychology, transpersonal psychology, and what is now termed "positive psychology," especially during the 1980s and his time as a lecturer at the University of Southern Maine. It is important, therefore, that for preservation of Tanous' thoughts, experiences, and research, and for historical purposes, this book now be available for all to read. This has been made possible thanks to the Alex Tanous Foundation for Scientific Research (Portland, Maine, U.S.A.) and its many goals, which include archival work of Tanous' legacy. Such goals were laid out in the establishment of the Foundation by Tanous in March 1990, shortly before his untimely death in July of that same year.

For those not familiar with Tanous, mentions of him are scattered throughout various literature on parapsychology. He is most noted for his alleged ability to travel mentally outside of his body and report back on his experiences (aka, an Out-of-Body Experience or OBE for short). He was tested for these abilities over a twenty-year period at the American Society for Psychical Research (New York, U.S.A.). Other noted abilities, which had received some research attention, included: premonitions, light projection from his eyes, and psychic healing—the latter ability having many overlaps with the subject of this present book. Tanous, along with the author Harvey Ardman, documented his experiences from early childhood to later life and his academic career in the autobiography entitled *Beyond Coincidence.*

It must be understood by the readers that this present book is a historical document, yet we feel the information contained within may be of importance to certain scholars, and of general interest to the public. The writings beyond this foreword do not necessarily reflect the views and procedures of modern research and therapeutic practices, as many changes have taken place in thirty years. Therefore, we wish to provide within this foreword, a brief outline of the current position of "clinical parapsychology" in relation to the therapeutic practices and seemingly "anomalous processes" that can be related to those discussed within this book.

Clinical parapsychology can be described as a branch of parapsychology where "if a client or patient is asking for professional help" regarding anomalous experiences then qualified parapsychologists or relevant professionals acquainted with parapsychological findings "evaluate these experiences and how to deal with them in a clinical, counseling and social welfare setting" (Kramer, Bauer, & Hövelmann, 2012, p.3). Alternatively, Tierney (2012) provides the following description, "'clinical parapsychology' can be viewed as a useful term that distinguishes a body of knowledge, distinct from the rest of abnormal psychology, which advocates psychotherapy (of various types) for distress caused by phenomena, which, in someone's judgment, are not only exceptional / extraordinary / anomalistic, but, in particular, within the purview of parapsychology" (p.247). Therefore, the clinical approach to parapsychology is concerned with the impact of an anomalous experience and/or process on a person, rather than on investigating the mechanisms behind the anomalous phenomenon itself.

When we say anomalous experiences, we are typically referring to human experiences and abilities that are either rare or that seem to sit outside of current scientific paradigms. The experiences are anomalous in that they may appear to be unusual to the experiment, or the processes involved appear to occur without any conventional explanation as to *how* and *why* they occur—i.e., spontaneous precognitive visions, witnessing apparitions of the dead, hearing voices with no apparent source, poltergeist type activity around the home, and so on. Upon investigation, many conventional explanations may arise, which could explain the experience. This is especially true of synaesthesia. The experience of "seeing sounds" or "hearing colors" is unusual but their explanations fit within current scientific paradigms. While parapsychology is interested in known psychological processes that make things appear unusual when, in fact, we can explain them (see French & Stone, 2014), it is also interested in cases where convention does not appear to apply. Parapsychologists engage in testing claims of anomalous processes among the general population or in rare cases, within specific individuals. Sometimes these claims can be attributed to known mechanisms such as coincidence, false memory, or misperceptions. Other claims, however, seem to fall outside of mainstream science's understanding of time, space, and energy.

These phenomena have received extensive and continued study from the field of parapsychology. It became established within the university setting at Duke University in the late 1920s thanks to the guiding work of Joseph Banks Rhine, Louisa Rhine, and colleagues. In 1969, the Parapsychological Association became an affiliate of the American Association for the Advancement of Science and still is to this day (Beloff, 1993; Horn, 2009). Today, a number of universities around the world—predominantly in the U.K.—deliver classes on parapsychology normally within the psychology curriculum, and have established research groups (the University of Northampton and the University of Edinburgh, for example), and support research degrees into parapsychology (see Carr, 2016; Irwin, 2013; Pratte, 2016).

In clinical parapsychology, it is often the case that counseling and psychotherapy are given to someone who has suffered some form of traumatic experience, in which anomalous processes may have been encountered—post-trauma. The counselor in these situations would either be skilled in parapsychological research and/or knowledgeable of parapsychological findings and, therefore, can sympathize with the patient and counsel them in the best possible manner. Such a process allows the patient to freely discuss the anomalous incident without fear of ridicule from the therapist, or having their experiences dismissed out of hand, or carelessly explained away as nothing more than a subjective hallucination as a result of post-traumatic stress—and not worth focusing on or discussing. Unfortunately, this has been the case for many people in the past who have encountered anomalous events in their lives—most typically during bereavement (Cooper, Roe, & Mitchell, 2015; Krippner, 2006). Clinical parapsychology has mainly focused on counseling and psychotherapy for reports of anomalous events. However, it can also involve alternative therapies in the process of healing (psychologically or physiologically), meditation in relation to mental health and anomalous experiences, and any other recognized overlaps between clinical psychology, alternative therapies, and parapsychology (i.e., personal health and well-being in relation to anomalous experiences and processes).

From examining the parapsychological literature, it can easily be argued that Tanous was a pioneer in the area of "psychic counseling." Early on, he realized that telepathy, clairvoyance, precognition, and similar phenomena were not necessarily delusions or pathological symptoms but a part of the human condition. The groundwork for this perspective had been laid by Eleanor Criswell and Laura Herzog in a 1977 article on the topic. They had established a psychic counseling center at Sonoma State University in California using a "client-centered" approach. The U.S. psychologist Carl Rogers introduced this approach. He focused on the client's experience, not the counselor's interpretation of that experience. Criswell and Herzog provided an atmosphere in which the client could integrate their psychic experience with their daily living. Even so, they emphasized the importance of working with a qualified counselor or therapist who would be accepting and non-judgmental. All too frequently, family members failed to believe, let alone support, a spouse or child who reported dreams about the future or picking up on the thoughts of someone in a different location.

Criswell and Herzog observed that not knowing where one's boundaries end and where another person's boundaries start can be disorienting. Psychic experiences sometimes become perplexing or frightening, but the skilled counselor or psychotherapist can help a client to assimilate them in a meaningful and positive manner. An attitude of unconditional positive regard conveys an acceptance free of evaluation and judgment, facilitating the development of trust. At the same time, the psychic counselor and psychotherapist needs to recognize when the reported experience is a symptom of severe mental disorder and arrange a consultation with a clinic or specialist for further evaluation and treatment.

In 1983, Arthur Hastings of the California Institute for Transpersonal Psychology (now Sofia University) described a pioneering counseling approach to parapsychological experiences. Hastings found that there was value in giving the experience a name; previous to counseling, the client might have ascribed the experience to "crazy thinking" or worse. Hastings also included reality testing in his work, helping clients differentiate between fantasy or wishful thinking and a psychic experience that was grounded in consensual reality. He noted that common reactions to a psychic experience were fear, dread, anxiety, and depression. But by creating a calm, supportive atmosphere, the counselor could turn those emotions into curiosity, appreciation, and wonder. Conversely, when people report anomalous experiences attributed to a deceased loved one, the vast majority of such experiences are reported to be positive and naturally enlightening in coping and recovery from grief (Cooper, Roe, & Mitchell, 2015).

Hastings placed considerable emphasis on symbolism, especially if someone had a dream about their imminent demise. The dream might call upon the dreamer to allow a dysfunctional part of them to die so that a healthier psyche could emerge. Symbolism might also explain intuitive impressions of past lives. In other words, not all psychic experiences are veridical, but might be of value regarding emotional processing and revising one's life's direction. Again, proper training is needed to help the counselor to be supportive and non-judgemental.

Stanislav Grof (e.g., 2012) has written many articles and books about "spiritual emergencies" and how they need to be differentiated from "spiritual emergences." For Grof, many symptoms considered to be "psychotic" are actually signs of a radical personality transformation. An "emergency" can be turned into an "emergence" with proper treatment and care. Past-life experiences, near-death experiences, spirit possession, and other "psychic openings" should not be the cause of knee-jerk medication but, in the hands of a skilled counselor or therapist, should be an opportunity for profound and long-lasting personality change. The American Psychiatric Association gave some recognition to this possibility in the fifth edition of its *Diagnostic and Statistical Manual of Mental Disorders* when it included spiritual and religious crises as a legitimate diagnostic term.

This book provides documentation of examples—to a large extent—of clinical parapsychology in action. However, as an example of clinical parapsychology and the application of psychotherapy to anomalous experiences, the processes described within this book are *reversed*. By this, we mean that an anomalous process is *applied* to help the various patients discussed, through a process of psychiatric or psychological help. While the patients themselves suffered with various life issues, they *did not* necessarily claim to have had anomalous experiences, at least not in relation to their problems for which they had sought psychotherapy. Instead of the traditional course of clinical parapsychology offering therapy to those who report anomalous experiences, Tanous used the psychotherapy setting to predict psychically the very root of each patient's problem, which was supported by the patient confirming various facts about their life through these readings. The psychiatrist involved, Elaine Schwinge, then used Tanous' *psychic diagnosis* to guide the best course of treatment.

It is this application of a psychic in the psychotherapy process, which makes the treatments and accounts described throughout this book so unique. It is something that still, today, would receive limited acceptance or approval in the professional health care setting, unless it were strictly conducted as an "alternative therapy" at the patient's request and permission. It is also, to some extent, how the manuscript of *Paranormal Psychotherapy* came about, given that so many people had sought Tanous' help and assistance, for his purported abilities of psychic healing (see Tanous with Ardman, 1976, pp. 79-89).

Was this technique unique? Apparently not; for example, in the 1960s a psychotherapist named Dr. Albin Gustafson, published an article entitled "I use ESP in psychotherapy." The article documented Gustafson's use of premonitions and dreams pertaining to his clients, which appear to be accurate, and were incorporated into the sessions and discussions with clients in their paths to recovery. He stated "it is my belief that the most important single process in psychotherapy may consist of both ESP [aka, extra-sensory perception; i.e. psi] and the direct influence of the therapist on the client's nervous system" (Gustafson, 1966, p.92). The difference between Gustafson's presentation against that of Tanous, is that Tanous produced an extensive account of this process, which is before you now. Not only is this documented from his perspective with various clients, but also with the input and advisement from a psychiatrist and psychotherapist who observed and incorporated his techniques into their standard practice.

There are several conventional explanations that we could apply to abilities seemingly being used by Tanous in this case. If we wanted to explore them on a parapsychological level, we would turn to his potential employment of cold reading and Barnum scripts of generalized information (Roe & Roxburgh, 2013). However, in this clinical setting, the important factor is that whatever technique or process he was applying—genuine or not—it appeared to work for the client and they were satisfied by the result. For positive psychologists, the application of positive intentions and motivational support featured within this manuscript may be of significant interest, especially in learning more about the impact of such on our health and well-being and the placebo effect.

We do hope that you enjoy this book and its historical value. In agreement with the Alex Tanous Foundation, only minor changes have been made, primarily where any original statements were grossly inaccurate regarding terminologies of psychology and general typographical errors. The original manuscript can be seen by request through the Alex Tanous Foundation or the Rhine Research Center. The only major change that has been made is in the title, which is now *Psi in*

Psychotherapy. The word "paranormal" carries with it various stereotypes, misunderstandings, and so-cial-stigmas. As such, science would typically favor the term "anomalous" phenomena. Tanous wished to convey that the processes involved in his abilities were still not fully chartered by science, and yet, we under-stand the processes involved as possibly being due to some form of psi. The blanket term of "psi" is used as a referent for all forms of parapsychological phenomena (i.e. extrasensory perception or ESP, psychokinesis or PK and survival (phenomena suggestive of the mind operating following death)). This usage is similar to the way "x" represents the unknown element in the process of algebra mathematics until identified. Therefore, the term "psi" has been used as a more direct referent of what Tanous, Schwinge and Bambrick (the authors), recount within this book regarding apparent psychic phenomena within the psychotherapy process.

Callum E. Cooper, Ph.D., University of Northampton, U.K.
Stanley Krippner, Ph.D., Saybrook University, U.S.A.

October, 2018

References

Beloff, J. (1993). *Parapsychology: A concise history*. London: The Athlone Press.

Carr, B. (2016). The legacy of Bob Morris for the Koestler Unit and beyond. *Mindfield, 7* (3), 97-102.

Cooper, C.E., Roe, C.A., & Mitchell, G. (2015). Anomalous experiences and the bereavement process. In T. Cattoi, & C.M. Moreman (Eds.), *Death, dying and mysticism: The ecstasy of the end* (pp.117-131). New York, NY: Palgrave Macmillan.

Criswell, E., & Herzog, L. (1977, January/February). Psychic counseling. *Psychic Magazine*, 6-13.

French, C.C., & Stone, A. (2014). *Anomalistic psychology: Exploring paranormal belief and experience*. London: Palgrave.

Grof, S. (2012). *Healing our deepest wounds: the holotropic paradigm shift*. Newcastle, WA: Stream of Consciousness Productions.

Gustafson, A. (1966). I use ESP in psychotherapy. *Fate, 19* (11), 86-93.

Hastings, A. (1983). A counseling approach to parapsychological experience. *Journal of Transpersonal Psychology, 15*, 143-167.

Horn, S. (2009). *Unbelievable*. New York, NY: HarperCollins.

Irwin, H.J. (2013). *Education in parapsychology: Student and instructor perspectives*. Gladesville, NSW: Australian Institute for Parapsychological Research.

Kramer, W.H., Bauer, E., & Hövelmann, G.H. (Eds.) (2012). *Perspectives of clinical parapsychology*. Bunnik, Germany: Stichting Het Johan Borgman Fonds.

Krippner, S. (2006). Getting through the grief: After-death communication experiences and their effects on experients. In L. Storm & M.A. Thalbourne (Eds.), *The survival of human consciousness* (pp.174-193). London: McFarland.

Pratte, E. A. (2016). Student corner. *Mindfield, 7* (3), 119-121.

Roe, C. A. & Roxburgh, E. C. (2013). An overview of cold reading strategies. In: C. Moreman, (Ed.), *The Spiritualist Movement: Speaking with the dead in America and around the world: Vol. 2, Evidence and beliefs* (pp.177-203). Santa Barbara, CA: Praeger.

Tanous, A., with Ardman, H. (1976). *Beyond coincidence: One man's experiences with psychic phenomena*. New York, NY: Doubleday.

Tierney, I. (2012). Clinical parapsychology in the United Kingdom. In C. Simmonds-Moore (Ed.), *Exceptional experience and health* (pp. 242-253). Jefferson, NC: McFarland.

PSI IN PSYCHOTHERAPY

PREFACE

~

This book represents the culmination of several years of research in the new field of "psi in psychotherapy." This term is used by Drs. Tanous and Schwinge to describe how they work to bring healing to emotionally troubled patients. Our objective is to present the reader with a practical treatment manual and with this end in view, we have selected five cases which represent the range of problems treated conjointly by a psychiatrist and a psychic.

In the 1960's there was widespread enthusiasm for interest in the paranormal. Interest in the paranormal gradually moved from isolated predictions about the future by psychics to a scientific environment in Duke University, the American Society for Psychical Research (New York) and the Society for Psychical Research (London). Scientific journals dealing with paranormal research have published on a frequent basis—in Europe, America and Canada—a number of scientific articles dealing with healing abilities of world renowned psychics. The healing activity was primarily concentrated on plants and animals.

Drs. Tanous and Schwinge focus their energies on healing the memories of troubled individuals. This unique team is distinguished by three qualities: empathy, telepathy and clinical wisdom.

Memory is always a paradox in one's destiny. Memories have multiple uses in our daily lives. They may be used as a shield to sustain the sharp biting frailties of daily struggles; as an irritant in repeating negative experiences from one's past, etc. Drs. Tanous and Schwinge direct their interventions on several different levels of the individual throughout the course of his/her therapy.

In a particular way our ability to deal effectively with memories imprisoned in our psyche is directly correlated with one's freedom and destiny.

The approach of this book explicitly deals with traditional psychiatry and psychic therapy. Because neither of these disciplines alone is sufficient, a genuine interdisciplinary approach was attempted while breaking fresh new ground, particularly in relation to parapsychology and psychotherapy matters.

Moments of significant insight are recorded in the consciousness of each patient in this book.

Last but not least, we are grateful to the pioneering efforts of psychical researchers and parapsychologists who have tirelessly sought to have psi experiments replicated in order to make credible our understanding of anomalous experiences and abilities that are commonly reported in day-to-day life. Most especially, we thank Dr. Karlis Osis, an eminent pioneer in the field of psychical research who steered Alex Tanous into being one of the principal experimental subjects at the American Society for Psychical Research.

INTRODUCTION

~

The ocean of psi within psychotherapy remains largely uncharted. The appearance of buoys and beacon lights to aid the mariners are all too rare. This book is an attempt to position a beacon light and lay buoys to guide mental health and psychic members of the ship's crew to a newly established port.

In decades gone by [the 1970s and before], the scientific community began to test the abilities of psychics under rigorous conditions. For the most part, their research has focused on the psychics' ESP abilities, accuracy in forecasting future events, and the healing of plants, animals and humans. Up to the point of this writing [the 1980s], there had been a conspicuous absence of articles and books on the efforts of the psychotherapeutic and psychic communities to collaborate in bringing relief to the emotionally ill.

The purpose of this book is to give an overview of an innovative approach in the combined fields of conventional and unconventional psychotherapeutic healing. The term we use for this approach is called "psi in psychotherapy." It signifies the joining of talents from the fields of psychotherapy and psychics.

Psychics held a prominent place in agrarian, and hunting and gathering societies. They were besieged with a myriad of requests from people wanting to know about future events such as crops, happiness, sex of their unborn child, meaning of dreams, communication with departed loved ones, and about survival after death. In those times, people had a view of oneness with the universe, as well as the importance of proper balance and harmony in nature as well as one's own life. They had an awareness of perennial cycles, a firm belief in a deity and spirits through nocturnal dreams, or of deceased persons who appeared in those dreams, and the forecasting abilities and healing abilities of psychics.

With advent of the Age of Reason in the West, psychic healers moved from a central to a peripheral position in society. The scientists sought to gain greater control over nature by scientific methodology and technology. The application of scientific principles and the use of mathematics to make accurate predictions regarding future outcomes were the two essential features of this age. Psychic claims made by non-conventional practitioners, for example, future forecasting and healing by touch or at a distance, were thought entirely to be exaggerations or deceptions. Humankind, the rationalists assumed, was governed by laws that consisted of substances that could be measured by quantitative means. This impression seemed accurate until the onset of the Second World War.

The splitting of the atom and its destructive release on the populace of Hiroshima and Nagasaki gave governments and their people pause to reflect on "What have we wrought?" The escalation of conflicts around the globe, the increase of membership in the nuclear club, and the growing awareness of all nations to a possible nuclear Armageddon have given rise to an introspective search for untapped abilities in the world of the mind to promote peace, harmony, and healing. Currently, 15 million Americans are affiliated with 500,000 self-help groups.[1] This recent megatrend away from an exclusive use of conventional healing procedures has been shaped by media spots and program specials regarding both the successes and limitations of mainstream medications and therapeutic interventions on

---

[1] Editorial Note: These figures as of 2018 are now exceptionally higher (into the millions) and are subject to a billion-dollar industry.

specific health problems. Also, the proliferation of self-help books promising mastery over everything from anxiety to zoophobia has become a steady diet of the average consumer in the recent decades.

Interest in anomalous human experiences and processes has soared in the last several years. Hardly a week goes by that an astrologer, psychic, or medium doesn't appear on a TV Talk Show. Astrological forecasts appear in daily and weekly newspapers. Various "Electronic Churches" boast of psychological and physical healing on a regular basis. Astrologers and persons claiming psychic gifts are listed in the yellow pages of local telephone directories. The popularity of "the paranormal" has given an air of respectability to some psychic practitioners and their art of unconventional healing. Unconventional healing has made incremental gains towards becoming a viable alternative to conventional healing. Conventional and non-conventional healers are like twins who were separated at birth by divorcing parents. The conventional healer was taught to hold in high regard analytical thinking, specific procedures, trial and error hypotheses, and measured outcomes in order to resolve human difficulties. Non-conventional healers were educated by their mentors in the development of high level intuition to help in their diagnosis and prognosis, and they often used "healing energy" to restore suffering individuals to health. Periodically, the divorced parents (psychic and mental health professionals) would inject a "pinch" of prejudice about "them" and a "dash" of sentiment of how it might have been. But now the time has come for conventional and non-conventional healers to join in a collaborated effort to bring relief to persons suffering emotional difficulties.[2] This book is an attempt to evaluate the contributions of the psychic and the psychiatrist in their efforts to heal patients.

The Authors, 1985
(Tanous, Schwinge, & Bambrick)

[2] Editorial Note: In the language of today, we would normally say 'alternative and complementary medicine' as opposed to 'non-conventional healers'.

CHAPTER 1

THE MEETING

~

A lex Tanous, a multi-gifted psychic, was born on November 26, 1926, in his grandparents' home in Van Buren, Maine. Both his parents were psychic. They chose to settle in Van Buren because it resembled their Lebanese village in terrain and climate. Alex was born with a veil, i.e., the water-bag that protected him in the womb was draped over his head and shoulders (also known as the afterbirth or embryotic sack). It was a Middle Eastern tradition, which holds that a child born with the veil is gifted.

In his left palm is the mystical cross, a straight vertical line crossed by two short horizontal creases. Linked to these lines was something more remarkable—the name "Alex" spelled out backward, quite clearly, in lines and creases. Before he was born, his parents had considered naming him after a grandfather Alexander. When they saw the palm of his hand, they felt that his name had been preordained. During his early childhood, Alex began to display psychic abilities. At eighteen months of age, he was able to pick out his favorite record, "Mary had a Little Lamb", from a stack of some fifty records by merely feeling the edges of the records until he came to his favorite. Having visions of things before they happened, and the ability to go "out of his body at will" and speak about where he had been and provide such details were also documented.

In adolescence, Alex was caught up in the snare of competing loyalties. On one hand, he desired to have his psychic gifts recognized and validated, while, on the other hand, his exposure to a very narrow interpretation of Catholicism left him with sharp guilt feelings when he exercised his psychic gifts. In high school, a science teacher encouraged Alex to explore the relationship between science and religion. He recognized Alex's psychic gifts and encouraged him to use the gifts he had received from God, and to ease up on his guilt trip.

After a tour of duty with the United States Army, Alex enrolled in college. His academic accomplishments include the following: a B.A. (Bachelor of Arts) from Boston College in history and government; M.A. (Master of Arts) in philosophy from Boston College;

M.A. in theology from Fordham University; M.Ed. (Master of Education) in counseling and guidance from the University of Southern Maine, and a D.D. (Divinity Doctorate) from the College of Divine Metaphysics in Glendora, California. He is also a certified school psychologist for the State of Massachusetts.

He has used his psychic abilities as a clairvoyant to help the police solve crimes, to make psychic diagnosis, to send healing energy to the physically ill, to send telepathic messages, and to predict future events with uncanny accuracy. He is in great demand as an international lecturer. He is co-author of two books, *Beyond Coincidence* and *Is Your Child Psychic?* [3]

Dr. Elaine Schwinge was born in Horicon, Wisconsin on January 14, 1920. She derived her interest and dedication to help the sick and suffering from her father. During her childhood he emphasized the necessity of treating the mind, body, and spirit of the person. She remembers most especially those private times with her father, including long walks, Saturday matinees at the movies, discussions about the world and one's responsibility to use talents and gifts for others.

---

[3] Editorial Note: Following his death in 1990 the third book by Dr. Tanous was released entitled *Dreams, Symbols and Psychic Power* and more recently, his incomplete book *Conversations with Ghosts* was edited and published in 2013.

Shortly after completing high school, Elaine entered the University of North Carolina, Chapel Hill, and she went on to graduate from medical school with a M.D. (Medical Doctorate). She completed her psychiatric residency at the United State Public Health Service in Lexington, Kentucky. For the next twenty-five years, she held a variety of positions with Federal and State institutions in the United States.

Eight years ago, she was diagnosed as having early colon cancer. She complied with the conventional healing approach of surgery and medication. Throughout her recovery process, she used her faith in God as a dominant resource. Members of her faith group would visit frequently. One of the members of the faith group had particularly warm hands. Dr. Schwinge remarked that her hands felt warm, and the woman replied that she had psychic healing abilities. From that point onwards, Dr. Schwinge decided to explore the field of psychic healing and the interest has been maintained to the present.

Dr. Schwinge had long been interested in the meanings of dreams. Her training had put her in good stead to interpret the symbolic meaning of her client's dreams. Since her recovery from cancer, she made an informal study of the place of dreams in the Bible as well as the use of dreams in the fields of psychology and parapsychology. She heard Dr. Tanous make a clinical presentation in Philadelphia, Pennsylvania, regarding alternative approaches to healing and dream interpretation.

Shortly after Dr. Tanous made his presentation, Dr. Schwinge introduced herself. She told him about her dream and desire to work with a psychic in her practice. She was impressed with his sensitivity, understanding, and compassion for the emotionally afflicted person.

In the beginning, the problems for establishing a working relationship seemed formidable. The first problem centered on attracting clients who were open to accept help from both conventional and non-conventional healers. Clients who would accept a psychiatrist and psychic working together have usually tried various traditional therapeutic approaches without obtaining desired relief. They did not rule out the possibility of being helped by a combination of conventional and non-conventional approaches and had not had serious philosophical differences with the general orientation to psychic healing.

The second problem was the conventional community healers' attitude—the mental health professionals—towards this innovative approach. Movement by conventional healers towards this approach has been somewhat slow. The recent exposure of psychics on talk shows, newspapers, TV specials, and public interest in psychic phenomena has left the conventional healers a little more inquisitive regarding the possible use of psychic input. Others showed signs of displeasure by facial grimaces and arched eyebrows when the topic was introduced in general discussion.

The third problem was to engage a colleague to monitor the non-conventional (psychic input) psychotherapeutic process, define terms, specify role functions of psychiatrist and psychic, and to articulate procedures to be employed at various stages of therapy. Dr. Tanous and Dr. Schwinge chose Dr. Andrew Bambrick for the task.

Andrew F. Bambrick, Ph.D. (Philosophy Doctorate), is a psychotherapist in private practice. For the past fifteen years, he has been heavily involved in teaching, training, and writing in the field of psychotherapy. He has been consultant to local, regional, State and National groups regarding psychotherapy issues.

His interest in parapsychology and anomalous experiences was sparked in the small American-Irish village of his birth. His family and extended family had a firm respect for "God-gifted people"—psychics—and saw them as helpers and healers.

CHAPTER 2

PSI VS. PSYCHOTHERAPY

~

Definitions and Purpose

Using psi processes within psychotherapy is an innovative approach in the field of conventional and non-conventional healing. It is a relatively short-term form of psychotherapy. Chiefly, it consists of a combined approach by a psychic and a psychiatrist—or psychologist or any other relevant health care professional—to promote the healing of genetic/childhood experiences in the memory of the troubled client and to increase their freedom and autonomy. The basic principle of such psychotherapy is that genetic / childhood experiences are the primary continuous source of influence on a person throughout life. The chief ingredients in this healing process are: the identification of dysfunctional genetic experiences in the client's memory; the transmission of healing energy (i.e. positive cognition/ thought); working through emotional difficulties, catharsis and subsequent insight.

Psi in psychotherapy is based on the premise that individual conflicts stem from a transmission of skewed genetic and/or childhood experiences.[4] It enables clients to cope more effectively with these dysfunctional experiences and to make maladaptive attempts in maintaining relationships. The term "psi in psychotherapy" indicates the use of conventional and seemingly anomalous yet recognized processes to bring relief to the suffering client. In primitive societies families having emotionally and/or physically ill members, sought out psychics in order to have them make a diagnosis and, where possible, heal the malady. Frequently, psychic healers asked the patient to follow a specific set of procedures in order to bring about recovery.

---

[4]   Editorial Note: This could be seen as a psychodynamic approach.

Misconceptions

During a recent lecture series on psi in psychotherapy, Dr. Tanous identified three major misconceptions. First, those imbued in non-conventional mental health services had pre-judged psi in psychotherapy to be a hodge-podge of techniques interspersed with persuasive gimmicks.

Dr. Schwinge uses the *Diagnostic Statistical Manual of Mental Disorders*, third edition, DSM-III.[5] There are five parts of a DSM-III psychiatric diagnosis. Each part is called an Axis. Each axis is numbered with a Roman numeral—Axis I, Axis II, Axis III, Axis IV and Axis V. Axis I refers to the part of the diagnosis used to describe the client's current episode or illness. Axis II is used to describe the styles or personality traits and disorders. Axis III describes current physical disorders. Axis IV focuses on the environmental stress the client is under. Axis V concentrates on the client's highest level of adaptive functioning in the areas of social relations, occupation, and leisure time activities. Dr. Schwinge is well grounded in analytic theory and therapy and utilizes this conceptual framework in assessing the client's conflicts on developmental levels.

---

[5] Editorial Note: Now its fifth edition (American Psychiatric Association, DSM-V, as of 2013).

Dr. Tanous shares a similar analytic orientation. To be sure, the persuasive factor of the psychic is important. He is in a key position to use his leverage to encourage the client to pursue a path, which will lead to the accomplishment of the client's personal goals. His interpretations of psychic impressions are always couched in sensitive and caring terms. Prior to making an interpretation, Dr. Tanous consults with Dr. Schwinge regarding the impact of the interpretation for the person's ego.

A second misconception is that psi in psychotherapy is weighted heavily toward the mystical and does not allow for insight or problem resolution. The assumption of the uninitiated within this field, is that the client will revert to a pre-Oedipal (also consider the Jocasta and Electra complexes) level by having the psychic act as a surrogate parent and that it will reassure him/her that all will be well in the future and one does not have to use struggle for insight and apply them to resolve problems and issues. The roles and functions of the psychic and the psychiatrist are sharply defined and balanced throughout the therapeutic process. For the most part, the role of the psychic is rather specific and time limited. Shortly after a full psychiatric evaluation has been made, Dr. Schwinge, with the client's approval, invites the psychic to make a diagnosis. Frequently, the patient experiences an initial catharsis subsequent to the identification of a dysfunctional genetic experience or scary traumatic experience. However, the psychic hastens to point out to the client that it is necessary to utilize the insights gained in therapy to resolve personal and interpersonal difficulties in his/her daily living.

Third, many assumed that the presence of a psychic as co-therapist would somehow minimize the importance of a client's relationship with the psychiatrist. The lines of demarcation are very clear with regard to the functions of psychic and psychiatrist. The psychic function is primarily time limited towards the initial evaluation phase of the therapy process, although he may be present as a co-therapist periodically throughout the middle and terminal phases of therapy. The role of the psychiatrist in the psi in psychotherapy process is an ongoing, trust-building relationship with the client. In the middle phase of therapy, the psychiatrist prescribes and adjusts medication and makes timed, interpretative statements in order to facilitate the client's growth. She affirms the client through verbal responses and caring gestures. When the client experiences periodic flare-ups, she introduces the client to self-relaxation techniques. Most often clients are capable of using self-relaxation techniques in their homes or on the job.

The psychic reinforces the psychiatrist's regimen with the client. Dr. Tanous works with Dr. Schwinge in developing procedures, strategies, refining goals and objectives, and articulating plans to enable the client to experience a sense of freedom and growth.

Drs. Schwinge and Tanous agree that it is important to establish a communal healing context. This context may be defined as the confluences of a motivated client, a psychiatrist with high level skills and abilities, and a credentialed psychic with healing energy.

Dimensions

Dimensions are avenues, which direct the therapist's focus on dysfunctional genetic and childhood experiences. There are four dimensions, which therapists use in the process of psi in psychotherapy. They are: the past, the individual, analogy and method. In focusing on the past dimension, Drs. Schwinge and Tanous assume that the origin of the individual's difficulties are anchored in the remote memory of the individual and concentrate on the client's internal events. Spouses, family members and significant others are not included in conjoint therapy sessions with the client. The therapist uses a set of procedures and techniques applied to every case. They assume that in order for the individual to grow, they must pass through stages of growth. Dr. Schwinge employs timed interpretations and Dr. Tanous transmits healing energy to provide an emotional catharsis for the conflicted individual. Analogies are used quite sparingly by both doctors in describing the client's growth processes.

Focus

The psychic focuses on (1) dysfunctional genetic and/or childhood traumatic experiences in the remote memory of the client; (2) relating current symptom clusters to previous unresolved conflicts transmitted across generations; and (3) stages in holistic integration.

Goals

The goals of psi in psychotherapy are: (1) the reduction of the client's anxiety; (2) the reduction of his/her symptoms; (3) improvement in trust-building relationships; (4) holistic integration.

Evaluation Phase

During the initial evaluation phase, seven tasks need to be completed by the psychiatrist and the psychic:

- Rationale for psi in psychotherapy (1)
- Assessment of the client's strengths (2) and weaknesses (3)
- Identification of dysfunctional genetic (4) and/ or childhood experiences (5)
- Initiate detoxification procedures for dysfunctional experiences (6)
- Determine client's readiness for change/healing (7)

Rationale for Psi in Psychotherapy

The therapist gives a brief explanation of the non-conventional psychotherapeutic process, procedures, and strategies, commonly used. The therapist then sets the schedule, specifies fees and educates the patient regarding the proper use of prescribed medication.

Assessment of Client's Strengths and Weaknesses

The psychiatrist makes an assessment of the client's social relationships with family, friends, their occupation functioning as an employee, husband, wife, student, and the intricacies of the tasks to be accomplished while maintaining those roles. Furthermore, the therapist explores the client's variety of interest and degree of involvement in hobbies and recreations.

Ascertain the Presence or Absence of Psychopathology

Dr. Schwinge utilizes the Minnesota Multiphasic Personality Inventory (MMPI), and/or other standardized tests to support her clinical impressions. Towards the end of the evaluation phase, the psychiatrist introduces the client to Dr. Alex Tanous, as psychic and co-therapist. His chief task is to identify the presence or absence of dysfunctional genetic experiences and/or childhood experiences.

Identification of Dysfunctional Genetic or Childhood Experiences

Dr. Tanous uses a twin-channeled approach in making an identification of dysfunctional genetic or childhood experiences. First, he makes an assessment of the colors in the client's aura. The aura may be conceptualized as a halo consisting of multi-colored emanation, which surrounds every human being. The aura has been called the emanation of the human spirit. He becomes aware of multiple psychological and/or physical problems within the client. In order to prioritize these problems he uses his clairvoyant and telepathic abilities to locate childhood and/or genetic memories within the client.

27

He relates to the client that he sees him/her in this particular setting—which then the client may confirm or dismiss. Dr. Tanous then selects the major genetic experience(s), which is causing the problem.

Readiness for Change

The therapist and psychic engage in a collaborative effort with the client to determine whether he/she is willing to undergo the inevitability of stress and uncertainty of working through conflicts successfully. Other factors used to determine the client's readiness to undergo changes are the client's ego, strength, viability, or relationships with family and others, the level of job satisfaction, the range of in-depth involvement in hobbies and recreational interests.

Process

The psi in psychotherapy *process* is divided into three parts (1) initial evaluation phase, (2) middle phase and (3) terminal phase:

Initial Phase

In the initial evaluation phase of therapy the reader is given an insider's view of the dynamics of the therapy sessions—as just outlined above. They will obtain perspectives on the clients (and their families) who have engaged in the psi in psychotherapy process. Furthermore, the reader will gain insight into the various procedures used to assess the client's strengths and weaknesses; to determine the presence of absence or psychopathology; to identify genetic and childhood trauma; to detoxify these traumatic experiences and to assess the client's degree of readiness for change.

Special emphasis is placed on the genetic and/or childhood experiences, which have predisposed the client to intermittent intra-psychical conflicts and concomitant maladaptive patterns of relating. Also, a review of the client's effective coping strategies is made.

Middle Phase

In the middle phase the reader can capture the reflections of the client's struggles as they attempt to develop meaning while working through conflicts, thus ennobling themselves in the process. The co-therapists help the client to identify obstacles for growth and development in his/her path.

The psychic's roles are employed briefly in this phase of the therapy. His chief function is to reinforce the initial treatment plan for the client. Frequently, in this particular phase of therapy, the psychiatrist makes timed interpretative statements in order to facilitate the client's growth. She affirms that if the client experiences periodic anxiety flare-ups, the psychiatrist will prescribe and monitor medicines and adjusts dosages as indicated. In addition the psychiatrist uses self-relaxation techniques in home, work and recreation contexts. Timed insights are crucial for the client in this particular phase of therapy in order to maintain his/her momentum for change. If the psychic is present in sessions during this phase of the therapy process, the client may attempt to short circuit the therapy process and forestall personal growth by asking the psychic a steady stream of "what if" questions. The conscious purpose of the client's strategy is to determine whether future rewards are worth their present effort. Drs. Tanous and Schwinge direct the client to symbolically roll up their sleeves and pursue their goals by turning their limitations into strengths. The client activates this strategy when they have had periodic setbacks or temporary loss of insight into the self. Sudden increases of optimism and awareness of personal growth are features associated with this phase.

Terminal Phase

In this, the third phase of therapy, the psychic and the psychiatrist review with the client their progress in the course of therapy. A review of the client's effective coping adjustment or medication is made. In the final session, the psychic and the psychiatrist seal the client's ability to manage his/her daily life by consolidating their gains and stressing the healing qualities and functions within the individuals living context.

It is our conviction that healing takes place among those who are related and relating. Each person has untapped healing potential to live a more integrated life. We place high value on the interconnection of human experience. In order to emphasize this belief, the therapist focuses on current or former problems that have not as yet had a healthy or healing solution. The therapists encourage the client to translate the solutions to his/her problem(s) so that they can have a potential resolution after therapy has officially terminated. The client must be able to apply these solutions in other settings such as home, job, and family. Finally, the therapist seals and labels the individual's newly found ability to live more productively.

CHAPTER 3

RELATIONSHIP OF BODY, MIND AND SPIRIT

~

The importance of balancing the body, mind and spirit relationship has become the central task of our personal survival. At the core of the balanced relationship is the healing we must have within ourselves so that we may find peace. Throughout my life's journey, I have searched for an understanding of how to balance these relationships within a healing perspective. From my life experience as a psychic healer, I have three basic assumptions regarding reality. First, energy is the fundamental building block of all our material and spiritual universe. This energy is capable of influencing us simultaneously on both the spiritual and material level. It is the essential connection between one's consciousness of the Spirit of God and His presence in our healing actions. The second is consciousness. Generally speaking, consciousness means being aware of one's internal events, e.g. thoughts, feelings, moods, fantasies, dreams, hopes, goals, and aspirations, as well as people and objects in our environment. However we are called to a higher consciousness, which I call spiritual consciousness. By spiritual consciousness I mean that divine or higher mind, which is present within humans and acts and guides each person toward higher levels of perfection in consciousness.

This Era of Humanity may apparently be called the Age of Genius or Higher Consciousness. The age of the genius is the age of consciousness. We are in what is called the era of the sacred consciousness—the spirit. I am not speaking about religion. I am speaking about you made holy—made whole—made alive. You are the individual who can walk on the earth and be able to handle situations around you, or help those who have less than you. Marx made us aware of the forces of the social consciousness. Freud made us cognizant of a personal unconscious. Jung introduced the collective unconscious and its psychic properties, but Jesus the Christ gave us the greatest consciousness and that is the Spiritual Consciousness. Spiritual Consciousness is that Divine or higher mind in man that becomes active and guides him as he reaches toward higher levels of perfection. Today we are seeking to make that consciousness explicit; however, it has always been with us in an implicit way. Many are blind to the higher levels of awareness and cannot see it. Only in the mode of spiritual consciousness will we be able to see the individual healed as a well as the total healing of the universe.

Today many are seeking to make spiritual consciousness, which had been implicit in their lives, decidedly explicit. Only in the attainment of spiritual consciousness can one fully appreciate the interaction of the individual and communal healing.

I like seminars which lift the consciousness of the group. When the seminar is over, group members take healing and information to their homes, jobs, and the larger community. The transmission of spiritual consciousness from one to another may be compared to the addition of spiritual links on an ever-lengthening chain. Pierre Teilhard de Chardin in his work *The Divine Milieu* coined a term "noosphere" to describe the evolutionary aspects of humanity's growing awareness of one another. Teilhard implied that as humans progressed further along the evolutionary scale, they would be able to communicate through a network of higher consciousness. I propose that healing and information channels are vibrant and dominant in the network of higher consciousness. One can tap into this network if one is in tune with God. The third assumption is universal oneness or community. Universal oneness is an omnipresent network. Its chief resources are healing and information. Altered states of consciousness are the key to tuning in to the network. When the individual has been able to bring a sense of balance in mind, body and spirit, they become a candidate to tap into the network of universal oneness.

Perhaps, an analogy between the physicist's search for a grand unified theory (GUT) and the psychic's search for an understanding of the relationship among humans, universal oneness may be useful. The physicist wants to understand how the universe runs, what it is made of, and how few laws are necessary to explain the whole of it. The psychic, on the other hand, does not seek to develop GUT but rather is selective in the use of the physicist's theories to give a rationale of how he knows, sees, influences, heals, etc. The debate between Universe and universe has been a constant, down through the ages. The Universe represents the things as they are in reality and the small universe represents our conceptualizations of the Universe.

Attitudes of the Healer

Humankind is called to participate in the process of healing. No one has the corner on healing. The medical doctor heals through medicine, and a mother heals by kissing the wound of her child. An animal licks the wound and it is healed. The tree bows its head and waits for the rain to run through it. There is no one who is not a healer in potential.

The attitude of the healer is a crucial ingredient in the healing process. If we are narrow-minded, or in real stress, or have a great deal of anxiety, then the spirit, the body, or the soul is not at ease. It is dis-eased, and it takes away from the power that is within us. Our attitudes and thoughts are not to be fixed and held bound by mechanical metaphors applied to human functioning and simplistic causality analysis. An attitude of openness, of the infinite consciousness of God and renewed faith in yourself needs to be maintained.

Spirituality is not limited to a particular religion. Higher consciousness is spirituality, and the power that lives within us is universal and, unless we can bring ourselves into the universal healing power of consciousness, then we cannot heal. You take away from that consciousness by desiring things that you do not need. If you really believe that you are a healer, you are a healer. We must be aware that some claim to heal beyond their belief and capacity. Healing can be achieved only through science and the mind—the full use of the mind that God gave us!

The second attitude is to learn how to utilize our spiritual consciousness to heal ourselves and make ourselves whole. The healing is not from me, the psychic, but rather it is because I am attuned to the consciousness of the Universe, to the heart and mind of God, and that lets the power flow through me and healing takes place. His healing power flows through every one of us in different degrees. We may adulterate that power when we believe that we are more or less than we are. We are channels of healing and information in the universal network of oneness and that oneness really means that everything is interrelated. If you isolate yourself from that consciousness then you will become ill and will have no power whatsoever.

You are the hands of God. You are the hands of the Spirit. It is that Universal healing power, that consciousness, the God power, which heals. With it, we heal each other. We are given this power to heal since the Master Jesus used it. He is the only Master I have known and I realize He is the channel of power given to us. I invoke His power when I send my healing energy to the physically ill. Sometimes I feel so unworthy at having been given these gifts. At other times I take comfort in the words from an inner voice that said, "Raise your head, my son, and make others realize that I live within them as I live within you. Be yourself and let Me be the One who works with you." For if we are conscious of love, then we are love and the power of love within us can say, like Jesus, "Thy faith has healed you."

My one and only teacher in healing is Jesus the Christ. He healed the sick, restored sight to the blind, and performed many other miracles. He encouraged His followers to love one another and minister to one another. Some of the cures that Jesus performed were brought about by the healing touch of His hands. At other times He healed from a distance and continues to heal in many ways.

Patient's Will to Live: Limitations on the Healer

From time to time, patients place limitations on the psychic healer. A number of patients use their will not to recover. Alfred Adler made us aware of the power instincts, which pulls one to death and life. One has but to look around and see the death instinct dominate the lives of many patients who consistently abuse alcohol, drugs, food; or maintain frenzied lifestyles; hang onto past hurts; plan future acts of revenge; level depressive sentences upon themselves. And others, through negative thoughts, hold on to the meager secondary gains, which are psychosomatic or life-threatening illnesses.

When it becomes obvious to me that individuals have their wills fixed and locked on not participating in their own healing process, I pray for them and turn my services to those who wish to participate in their healing process.

During the past four years I have made hundreds of psychic evaluations of the memories of clients suffering from emotional and mental illnesses. Memories, traumas, genetic and inherited consciousness are some of the significant areas, which I explore in my initial evaluation of a client's life.

In case after case, the memories of clients contained not only the early and subsequent memories of parents and grandparents, but also the parents' and grandparents' patterns of wrestling with problems, unfinished business, etc. During my search of the psychology literature for an understanding of how we can know things without actually having had the personal experience, I found the writings of Carl Jung most helpful. In his *Theory of the Unconscious* he gives both clinical and psychic insights when he states that, "We inherit a wisdom and experience without ourselves having had the personal experience."

We have all had the experience of being introduced to a concept or an idea for the first time and to have had the impression that, "I must have heard this somewhere before and forgotten about it. Now I am just being re-acquainted with the idea or concept." Quite frequently an investigation bears out the fact that we did indeed hear about this concept for the first time. However, we seemed to have inherited a wisdom that we had been acquainted with the concept in the distant past. Again, almost everyone involved with his family genealogy tree will identify past relatives as having certain talents, which were passed on from one generation to another. History is replete with families that have spawned a series of generations of highly talented persons in the arts and sciences. It is no mere coincidence that these talents emerge after having been dormant for several generations.

I believe that the lived experiences of our parents and grandparents are transmitted in genetic memory cells much as the inherited propensities, talents and vulnerabilities are coded in our genes.

Core Concepts: Genetic Memory and Inherited Consciousness

Genetic memory and inherited consciousness are the basic building blocks of the psychic system. "Genetic Memory" is a living repository of experiences from the birth of consciousness. It comes into existence when the first sentient impulses are recorded within the foetus. The psychic, in an altered state of consciousness, tunes in to this living repository in order to make an assessment of the presence of dysfunction. A similar assessment is made of the client's inherited consciousness.

Inherited consciousness is an intergenerational legacy of parental/grandparental propensities, vulnerabilities, and talents. Inherited consciousness has two sides. On one side is creativity, insight, vision and understanding, and, on the other, the unfinished business of parents and grandparents. Inherited consciousness like the unconscious has a life of its own. The psychic telepathically communicates directly with the inherited consciousness. If the latter side dominates, remedial attention is needed in order to halt the intergeneration legacy of unfinished business. When the legacy has been halted, the client no longer has the need to perpetuate loyalty for the unfinished business of parents/grandparents. At this point, the client is in a favorable position to work through the unconscious conflicts with the psychiatrist.

At the risk of sounding repetitive, the role of the psychic in psychotherapy is to communicate telepathically with the client's genetic memory and inherited consciousness. Genetic memory and inherited consciousness have an independent life of their own and exert powerful influences on one's consciousness.

Now let us turn our attention to the phenomenon of transmission of psychic healing energy across great distances. Theories abound regarding the transmission of energy. I present to you four cases in which energy was transmitted and patients recovered.

In subsequent chapters we will present five anecdotal cases, which describe how a psychic and psychiatrist in conjoint use their abilities to bring healing to emotionally ill people.

CHAPTER 4

DR. ALEX TANOUS
AS A HEALER

~

Since 1970, Dr. Tanous has had his psychic abilities and his ability to transfer energy tested by using rigorous scientific experiments.

As a psychic, Dr. Tanous has been repeatedly tested by Dr. Karlis Osis of the American Society for Psychical Research and all his work has been documented. Dr. Osis says: "He is a superstar in the field of psychics."

Others who have tested his healing energy are: Dr. Robert Miller, an industrial research scientist whose doctorate is in chemical engineering. Dr. Joel Whitton, a medical researcher in Canada, did extensive testing using the EEG and other equipment to measure the amounts of energy produced by his brain at different frequencies. He was also tested by Dr. D. Terracina of Columbia Presbyterian Medical Center. All the tests conducted showed Dr. Tanous as having significant results.

The tests showed that he was in an altered-state when the healing began and that it is possible to be very effective when sending the healing energy at a distance, as well as by touching a person. In the early testing, he worked with wilted plants and brought them back to life. After further testing he began to work with sending his healing energy to people who were physically ill.

At this point, the reader may be asking how can this happen? What is its destination within the other person? Dr. Tanous hypothesizes that it is directed towards the genetic memory. Perhaps Dr. Scott Peck can shed some light in this particular area for he states: "Recent scientific experiments with genetic material in connection with the phenomenon of memory suggests that it is indeed possible to inherit knowledge, which is stored in nucleic acid codes within the cell. The concept of chemical storage of information allows us to begin to understand how the information potentially available to the human mind might be stored in a few cubic inches of brain substances."

It is entirely possible that the energy emanating from the psychic healer triggers the agents within the genetic memory to set into motion a plan to destroy the disease and restore the body to health. This inherited memory has been passed down by countless previous generations of genes.

The following cases give testimony to his ability to transmit healing energy by touch or from a distance. Four cases of physical healing have been selected for inclusion in this chapter in order to show the progression of Dr. Tanous' work from physical healing to mental healing. Two of the four cases include patients who were diagnosed as having incurable cancer.

Taken from Four Documented Cases of Healing

A Cancer Patient

In November 1976, Raymond requested that Dr. Tanous come to see his father-in-law who had been diagnosed, the previous March, as having cancer of the lung, the base of his tongue, progressing into his stomach and probably into his brain. He was very ill and had been given only a year to live by three different doctors. Dr. Tanous went to see him and laid his hands on him. For the next five days his condition seemed to have gotten worse, but, a week after, he started getting stronger and stronger and his appetite came back. His general health and mental attitude was remarkably improved.

He had been receiving cobalt treatments since the original diagnosis was confirmed by exploratory surgery. The surgery was not able to correct the disease and radiation was only used to buy time with no hope for a cure.

This report was given seven months after his allotted year had passed and he was continuing to improve and resume normal activities and no signs of the cancer are apparent at the time of this report.

Candy's Case

Candy reported on her healing to an audience attending one of Dr. Tanous' lectures in June, 1979. The following was taken from her statement.

She reported that she had been in a very serious car accident, followed by surgery on her spine. She was partially paralyzed from the waist down for a while and had been almost totally blind for the last five and one-half months. She went from one specialist to another for the many different complaints, until one doctor found that she had a tumor on the pituitary gland. They told her that there was nothing, really, that could be done. The operation was too risky—and it was most likely that she wouldn't survive it. So they gave her a book on "Death and Dying."

She had taken some of Dr. Tanous' classes at the university and friends encouraged her to ask him for help.

She went up to Alex in the hall as he finished a class, and asked him if he would heal her. He said: "yes." She said: "well, when do we start?" He just hugged her and said: "I already did."

Alex told her that he conceptualized the healing scenario in the following way. "When I send my healing energy into the ill person his/her symptoms become exacerbated within a short period of time. In fact, they frequently mimic the final stages of the disease. Then the healing switches within the person are activated and the disease turns on itself, thereby giving way to recovery.

Candy reported that shortly after Alex had given her energy, the symptoms of her disease increased in intensity. Her physician increased medication to ease the pain. Laboratory tests were conclusive that the disease was in its final stages. However, within a week, she had undergone another series of tests to satisfy the clinician's curiosity that the tumor had disappeared. She was elated and said: "The Lord used Alex to heal me."

Another Automobile Accident

Paul reported that the vertebra in his fifth lumbar region was severed from his spine due to an automobile accident. The doctors would not operate because there was a 90% chance of leaving him in a wheelchair. He was given medication and exercise to help control the pain but nothing they did really helped and three years had passed. He attended one of Dr. Tanous' healing sessions and the pain left suddenly. He told Alex: "The pain left. There is no pain. My legs don't hurt. My back doesn't hurt." Alex told him to go back to his doctors and let them check to see what happened.

He reported that the doctors took new x-rays and couldn't believe the difference when they compared them to the old x-rays. They wanted to know what happened and Paul told them that: "Alex used his energy to fuse my back together again and it was spontaneous." One doctor said: "You are a very lucky person. There is somebody up there who loves you." Paul said: "I know that the healing came from Alex, but I know that God directed the healing."

A month later Paul reported that it was not just his back that was healed, but his spirit, his consciousness—and that he was healed "physically, spiritually, and mentally."

He Helped Edie and Her Mother too

Edie was in Dr. Tanous' class and when she left for school one evening she was not sure that her mother would make it through the night. Her mother was 88, bed-ridden for over a month, didn't know anyone and had to be fed. Edie asked Alex for help in healing her. When she arrived home that night her mother had walked downstairs and sat in her rocking chair waiting to greet Edie when she came home from class. Her mother continued to improve and was soon walking a mile a day on the beach. The doctor reported she was in the best condition they'd seen for a long time.

Edie's glasses had become a problem and she decided to change them for contacts and went to her optometrist. He found evidence of a detached retina in her right eye and recommended a specialist. Again, Edie asked Alex for help and the next day the specialist gave her a clean bill of health after a three and one-half hour examination. Her optometrist prepared to fit her with contacts but warned that the right eye wouldn't do as well, but when he tested it, he was amazed to find that she had 20/20 in her right eye.

CHAPTER 5

SPRING FORWARD AND FALL BACK

~

Ted's case is an exception to the time-limited, psi and psychotherapeutic approach. He was engaged in therapy with Drs. Schwinge and Tanous for a period of two and a half years totaling forty-seven sessions.

In the fall of 1975, Ted, a fledgling freshman, found himself in a very low mood during the first five weeks of the semester. In order to lift his spirits, he thought that a drive in the country might help. While Ted was on his way to the country, a small child darted out from between two parked cars into the street. Ted turned the wheel of his car while trying to avoid hitting the child, but the child was killed instantly.

After the police had made some preliminary investigations, Ted was released on his own recognizance. He went to his parents' home and withdrew emotionally from everyone. His parents, at Ted's request, made the necessary arrangements to disenroll him from college.

During the following months, Ted continued to have problems. His parents claimed that they had a communication problem with him. Ted began to abuse alcohol and marijuana on a frequent basis. When asked about his plans for the future, he responded with "everything is up in the air."

He developed a pattern of staying in bed until late afternoon on an average of four times a week. Shortly after rising in the mid-afternoon, he would eat a large brunch. Then he would proceed to become irritable and outbursts of explosive behavior followed.

Ted had a modest checking account, which was replenished by his parents. Frequently he became embroiled with bank personnel regarding the issue of cashing checks without sufficient funds. Ted had begun to make trips to nearby cities for several days at a time. The reasons for his comings and goings were shrouded in mystery and uncertainty. His family and friends were confused and puzzled about his rather unpredictable absences.

Family History

His paternal grandfather died when Ted's father, Richard, was only four years old. Richard had described his childhood as short-lived. His mother had encouraged him to become "the little big man" around the house. She encouraged him to develop a sense of responsibility in the performance of household duties. He and his mother became inseparable.

During adolescence he remained devoted and solicitous towards his mother. Shortly after his graduation from high school, he met a young, attractive girl named Bridget, two years his senior. They were married less than a year after their first date. His mother resented Bridget bitterly for taking her son away from her. Richard's mother moved out of her spacious twelve room Victorian home to an apartment, which was moderately furnished. There she promptly proceeded to ingest large quantities of alcohol on a daily basis. Heretofore, she had been reported to have been a moderate drinker. Within three years she died from cirrhosis of the liver.

When Ted was four years old, his maternal grandfather died of lung cancer. He has very sketchy memories of this grandfather. He remembers that his grandfather was left-handed. Also that he wanted his son, Frank, to take over the plumbing business when his tour of duty in Vietnam was finished.

Frank, Ted's uncle, was a member of the military police in the early phase of the Vietnam war. He wrote home frequently and said that he could not wait until he could take over the business end of the plumbing business.

While on patrol in Saigon, Frank had a fatal accident. The jeep he was riding in was destroyed by a land mine. He died in a hospital near Saigon a few hours later. Frank's father stood up under the ordeal of the funeral. He received the folded American flag and his body winced as the military escort squeezed off several rounds as a salute to their fallen comrade, and his knees buckled. He received family support during the playing of taps at the graveside. Shortly after he returned from the interment, he slipped into a deep depression. His grief remained unresolved until his death some four years later.

Evaluation Phase

Ted is a twenty-six year old Caucasian male with a muscular 6'2" frame. He has deep-set dark eyes and a face highlighted by a thick black Thomas Magnum-styled moustache. Prior to his involvement in therapy with Dr. Schwinge, he had been in therapy with several other psychiatrists for a period of seven years. They, too, classified him as a manic-depressive.

Ted was referred to Dr. Schwinge by a general physician in the Allentown area. The physician suggested to Ted that he considered placing himself under psychiatric care.

He had recently moved into the Allentown area from a nearby cosmopolitan city. His exit from that area had been somewhat dramatic. Ted had an altercation with the metro police and was subsequently arrested on charges of assault and battery, possession of illegal substances, resisting arrest and hitting a police officer. He was sentenced to 30 days in the municipal jail and a fine of $200 was imposed. Upon his release from jail, Ted made an appointment with a psychiatrist to obtain medication to help with his problems. Ted informed the psychiatrist that he had felt that he had to leave the metropolitan area.

Ted's manic-depression illness became manifest when he was nineteen years of age. His current issues included: problems with alcohol, marijuana abuse, the tendency to discontinue medication, minor surgery on his upper lip and a two pack a day smoking habit for ten years. He did not give evidence of the suicide ideation.

Dr. Schwinge asked Ted his feelings and opinions concerning unconventional healers. Ted said that he was open to explore alternatives and/or concomitant approaches to the healing of emotional ills. He had some basic knowledge of ESP findings and various reports of psychic claims. Dr. Schwinge made a clinical judgement that Ted possessed sufficient ego strength to profit from the psychic insight of Dr. Tanous. Ted was pleased with the possibility of finding out more about his early development. Dr. Schwinge explained the basic concept and general procedures, which Dr. Tanous used in his practice of psi in psychotherapy.

Psychic Evaluation

Dr. Schwinge introduced Ted to Dr. Tanous after the fifth session of therapy. Ted gave Dr. Schwinge permission to give Dr. Tanous two basic bits of factual information regarding himself. She told Dr. Tanous that Ted had a manic-depressive disorder and that currently he was being maintained on medication.

Dr. Tanous asked Ted to situate himself comfortably in the large chair. Ted had been directed by Alex to let his hands drop to his sides. Then he was told to close his eyes and slow his breathing.

Dr. Tanous put himself in an altered-state. He identified the significant colors in Ted's aura. Alex picked the thin glow of Ted's aura as an indication that healing was needed. Then he used his clairvoyance to obtain information regarding the sources of vulnerability.

Alex supplied Dr. Schwinge and Ted with data regarding the depressive tendencies of his parents and grandparents. This information correlated highly with the information, which Ted has disclosed to Dr. Schwinge in previous sessions.

Dr. Andrew Bambrick was an observer in this particular session and was impressed with the accuracy of Dr. Tanous' details regarding Ted's parents and grandparents. Prior to this session, Dr. Schwinge and Dr. Bambrick agreed to empty their minds consciously of details regarding Ted's family members. Dr. Tanous did not have access to the client's chart prior to this therapy session.

Three main points of Dr. Tanous' psychic assessment were:

1. Inherited genetic vulnerability for a manic-depressive disorder.
2. Indications that maladaptive familial patterns are present in Ted's genetic memory and exert an influence on his problem-solving activities and negotiations in interpersonal relationships.
3. A need to build a window of hope for Ted following his struggle for balanced mood.

Ted was amazed with Dr. Tanous' psychic ability to ascertain, very quickly, genetic vulnerabilities in his grandparents. He was doubly pleased that Alex had predicted his future success in accomplishing his projected goals. Ted asked for periodic assistance in dislodging maladaptive familial patterns and enhancing growth-producing patterns.

At the end of the initial evaluation phase of therapy, there was a mutual agreement to strive for the following goals:

- Control his mood swings by taking prescribed medication.
- Use psychic insights to better understand himself.
- Search for antecedents to his drinking and marijuana abuse.
- Lose one pound of body weight per week until normal body-weight was achieved.
- Obtain secure employment.
- Establish a viable and enduring relationship with a woman.
- Own his own home.
- Join "smoke enders."
- He would send for college catalogues and continue his education.

Middle Phase

The six areas of concentration for Ted and the co-therapists were: the guilt and grief feelings over the accidental killing of the young child, making connections with grandparents' legacy, stabilization of mood, development of viable relationship with a girl, increase frustration tolerance at the work place, and the pursuit of courses in higher education.

Dr. Schwinge explored the harsh aspects of Ted's superego. The superego may be viewed as an active repository for the commands and prohibition of parents and authority figures. It frequently functions as a primitive judge, jury and executioner for the person. When the individual does not have adequate freedom and autonomy he/she frequently suffers from an overload of "must" statements regarding individual conduct. The superego is relentless in its pursuit of balancing the scales of right and wrong in one's thoughts, feelings and actions. It is not a respecter of mitigating circumstances or individual vulnerabilities and it is most noticeable when an individual determines that his/her conduct was correct when given a particular set of circumstances and suddenly he/she has the thought: "you got away with it this time—however, next time...."

Dr. Schwinge worked with Ted rather intensely in getting him to make the connection between his lack of intention to be destructive towards the child and the consequences, which followed when his car ran over the child. On several occasions, Dr. Tanous was present with Ted and Dr. Schwinge and he sent healing energy to detoxify these painful memories.

What effect, if any, does the healing energy have on an individual? The mode of action and impact on various organs in the body and receptive centers in the brain is unknown at this time. Drs. Schwinge and Tanous are hopeful that their future research into the effects of the healing energy upon grieving individual will be able to be scientifically demonstrated in a way similar to the research with individuals who have depressed T cell function at five weeks following bereavement. It is interesting to note that T cell function was not present at two weeks. The T cells, lymphocytes originally derived from the thymus gland, mediate cellular and delayed hypersensitivity reactions. It may very well be that healing energy, imparted by a psychic, follows predetermined biological rhythms in the body and that the energy has a built-in wisdom of shutting certain switches on and off at various receptor sites in the body.

Grandparents' Legacy

Dr. Tanous traced Ted's grandparents' legacy of withdrawal when they suffered an emotional loss. He helped Ted to look at his past behaviors, which were self-destructive—his drinking, marijuana abuse, minor automobile accidents subsequent to the death of the child—as unconscious attempts to maintain the legacy of actions, which were passed on to him by his grandparents. Alex instilled hope in Ted by reassuring him that genetic vulnerabilities like genetic memories can be modified.

Drs. Schwinge and Tanous made a series of interventions in therapy sessions designed to enable Ted to become more aware when he made decisions, which were made independent of the legacy. In other words, Ted was acting independently when he purposely planned his future actions without the need for instant gratifications, and not because he only wanted to accomplish the task quickly. At other times he could abandon the task altogether and take full responsibility for the consequence of his actions.

Unresolved Grief

Alex approached the unresolved grief in the area of the accidental killing of the young boy, very sensitively. He compared the uncovering of this lingering hurt to a patient's gingerly peeking under the bandages with one eye partially open. Alex guided him to lift the edges of the bandages slowly.

Under Drs. Schwinge and Tanous' guidance, Ted immersed himself in the pain and fear of the accident. In several sessions he relived parts of the traumatic experience.

Alex helped Ted to translate his multiple minor car accidents and periodic abuse of alcohol and marijuana subsequent to the accident as self-administered destructive actions geared to assuage his guilty feelings. He prescribed the doing of good deeds for small children in Ted's neighbourhood as an effective means to reduce the concomitant aspects of his guilty feelings.

Ted possessed sufficient strength to review the painful memories of the accident and demonstrated an ability to endure the pain of guilt and grief. These painful memories have been detoxified significantly and he has relinquished his conscious attachment to them. He remains, however, quite cautious while driving his car.

Stabilization of Mood

For eighteen months, Ted's mood cycle followed the proverb of "spring forward and fall back." His biological clock would escalate to the high range with the emergence of spring. By late summer he would be in a high mood. In the fall he would drop to the low range and remain there throughout the long winter months. At the end of the eighteen-month period his mood became more stabilized. He was not subject to the ebb and flow of his genetic inheritance. Ted was vigilant about complying with prescribed medication and increased his confidence in the healing energy of Dr. Tanous. He reported positive benefits following the transfer of psychic energy from Dr. Tanous.

College Courses

Ted needed a little encouragement to send for college catalogues. He recited a series of self-imposed limitations when Dr. Schwinge explored his feelings about finalizing his decision to return to college. He would toss out: "I'm too old to return to undergraduate school. The students might not like me. What if I'm not smart enough to keep up? Suppose I flunk? What would happen if I were to get serious with a girl? I wouldn't be able to finish school and support a wife at the same time."

Dr. Schwinge helped Ted to face some of his fears about failure. First, he was instructed to imagine what his response would be if the fears would be realized.

Second, he was given homework assignments, which dealt with generating alternatives to coming to negative conclusions based on insufficient data. Third, he gradually began to demonstrate an ability to interrupt the chain of automatic negative thoughts and conclude by inserting pauses, then he would jot brief notes regarding his progress in coming to a conclusion. Slowly, he began to realize that he had time on his side when making decisions. He started to make constructive use of these pauses in his reflections on how his decisions were made. Quite frequently he would say: "In the past I started my problem solving process with a negative conclusion and I now proceed with a more positive approach."

Work

Ted had three jobs within a two-year period. For a period of two months he was employed by a local printing company. He started the job in late spring. Within a few weeks he began to feel euphoric and found that he would attempt to do too many things at one time on the job. His employer would point out his deficiencies and demand that he pay more attention to his work. After some particular shouting match Ted was fired.

He took the next few months off and resumed his search in the fall. This time he landed a job with an advertising firm. His boss, a hard-driving man with mediocre talent, took an automatic liking to Ted. During this honeymoon period, Ted made several excellent suggestions and his boss was given credit for the ideas.

As Ted's biological clock began to slow down, he became rather lethargic. His boss accused Ted of being lazy, uncooperative and unfair to the other employees. His boss needed new ideas to solidify his position with his immediate supervisor. Ted understood this and became resentful because he had not been given credit for his previous ideas and was unwilling to be pressured to produce a stream of new ideas on demand for his boss.

One afternoon his boss told him that the company was cutting back on personnel and he would be let go by the end of the week.

Ted landed his third job within two months as a part time assistant with a heating and air conditioning company. This type of work was more to his liking. He had an opportunity to learn new skills, offer suggestions and have them given due consideration. He enjoyed the variety, which the job offered. He held this job until he entered college on a full-time basis.

A Wanted Relationship

Ted began dating Robyn shortly after entering therapy with Dr. Schwinge and Dr. Tanous. Initially, Ted enjoyed dating Robyn. In his words: "She placed no demands on me." In the initial dating phase Robyn had been overly complimentary, reporting that they had so much in common. They enjoyed a similar appreciation of food, entertainment, sports and music. Frequently, he would remark that "It is so easy to be in love." Their mutual projections reached the zenith during this phase of the relationship.

As their relationship intensified, Ted began to have increases in anxiety whenever he felt pressured to increase the level of his commitment to her. Ted began to notice differences in himself and Robyn. Negotiations were more difficult. He became aware of some of his strengths and limitations in his ability to negotiate. Both he and Robyn decided to move in together. The new exposure to each other on a daily basis gave them opportunities to adjust to each other's needs.

Prior to announcing their engagement, Ted and Robyn had broken the relationship off on three occasions. He went through a period of self-doubt. Later he started to shed some of the "musts" regarding the way a relationship is supposed to be and was able to make a more harmonious settlement of their difficulties.

Final Evaluation

In this phase Ted had to simplify his lifestyle. His part time job barely covered rent and food. Robyn was bringing in the major share of their total income. The role reversal was difficult for Ted to handle. He had been raised to view a man as the primary breadwinner in the relationship. Robyn's assertiveness, at times, became irritating to his pride.

On another level he began to be more appreciative of Robyn's love, support and caring. For the first time in his life, he reported that he felt that he mattered to someone.

Currently, Ted is enrolled at a university within the Philadelphia area. His major is mechanical engineering. He reports a significant increase in his ability to concentrate on his academic subjects. Although his income is limited, he has been able to make adjustments and live within a fixed budget. He plans to marry Robyn, his girlfriend of two-years, in July of 1984.

Ted has shown a recent interest in computers. He is quite animated when discussing their usefulness in engineering. He is still being maintained on medication.

Ted has eliminated smoking from his life. He is not sure how this has happened. He attributes the information, which he received from "smoke enders," as having provided him with an incentive to discontinue the habit. Ted has drastically reduced his intake of alcohol. He says he can begin to feel things inside of himself and he doesn't have to drink to feel that something.

CHAPTER 6

A PINCH OF SUGAR

~

Lois is a forty-three year old married woman. She is considerably overweight. Recently she has become aware that she has been unable to shake off her feelings of depression. With some encouragement from her husband and friends, she sought out a psychiatrist. During the initial visit she wore a bright orange top and matching slacks. Her appearance was neat and clean. She wore a small crystal suspended on a gold chain around her neck. After the initial pleasantries were exchanged, Lois began to explain to Dr. Schwinge what had been going on inside her. She stated that she lacked energy; experienced occasional restlessness; and found herself crying for no specific reason. She admitted that she had no serious thoughts of suicide.

On a physical level, Lois has been having problems with irregular menses for the past several months. Her sinuses have become inflamed and a recurrent problem with a right inner ear infection has returned. Lois has been a binge eater for the greater part of her life. Periodically, she will exceed as much as eighty pounds her normal body weight. Having attained this weight level, Lois will utilize one of the many fad diets to bring her close to her normal body weight.

When Lois is in the high weight gain phase, her husband criticizes her, belittles her in front of the children, and over-indulges the children with affection and gifts. She feels that she is the lowest person on the totem pole where her husband's affection and support are concerned.

The preliminary diagnosis at the time of the first interview was as follows:

- Depression and anxiety.
- Sinus infection and right inner ear infection.
- Obesity.

Lois continued with her family physician to clear up her sinus and inner ear infections.

Family History

Lois is the younger of two siblings. The earliest memories of her parents are positive and friendly. Her mother, at age 42, died suddenly while housecleaning. Lois, 12 years old at the time, was summoned from school. After the funeral, Lois took her grief and worked on it in silence. Ralph, her brother, and four years her senior, was very protective of her during her period of grief. He also extended his protective arm to her throughout her high school years.

Her father began dating women about a year after his wife's death. Lois was a little jealous at first that her Dad was being unfaithful to Mom's memory. Sometimes she would resent the other women who wanted to take Mom's place in the home. At other times, she was happy that Dad was getting out to meet other women.

Lois had watched him date a number of women for five years following her mother's death. Then he began to spend a larger portion of his time with Bridget. Lois didn't make very much of this at the time, for it was her senior year in high school and she was caught up with attending the games, school, doing her homework, and have crushes on boys from a distance. Suddenly Dad announced that he was going to marry Bridget.

The entrance of Bridget, the stepmother, into the family was quite upsetting to Lois and Ralph. Her father permitted his new wife to set all the family rules. For example: she set the curfew time, screened their friends who came to visit, etc. They protested Bridget's power over them. Their requests for periodic negotiations of family rules had gone unheeded by the father. Gradually, Ralph began to put greater emotional and physical distance between himself and his father and stepmother.

Prior to dating her husband, John, Lois lost a considerable amount of weight and reached normal body weight for the first time in years. John was slightly overweight when they first started dating. After a few dates, he admitted that he, too, was on a perennial diet. Their dating activity was limited to quiet walks around familiar surroundings of her neighbourhood, sitting on the couch in her parents' home watching TV and very infrequently going out for dinner in sparsely crowded restaurants at off-peak hours. Lois describes herself as shy and afraid of crowds and fearful of new surroundings. This problem will be dealt with at greater length during the middle phase of the therapy.

Lois enjoyed her father's infrequent visits to her home, but he died two years ago. He was 78 years of age. She and her husband and brother flew to Florida for the funeral. This grief experience was exacerbated by two incidents. In the first incident, Bridget accused Lois of taking her dead mother's jewellery before she married Lois's father. Lois was shocked but considered Bridget on the verge of senility. The second incident revolved around obtaining transportation to the airport. They had assumed that the physician, Lester, Bridget's son from a former marriage, would drive them to the airport. He did not show at the appointed time. Fifteen minutes later an elderly couple said that they had been asked to provide transportation for Lois and family to the airport. These incidents acted as obstacles in her attempts to fulfil her father's request to respect Bridget. No further contact has been made by either side of the blended families. It would seem that an emotional cut-off has taken place.

Since the funeral, Lois has contacted her brother on several occasions. She claims that he and his wife have a high life style in Manhattan. They are interested in art, theatre, etc. On weekends, they spend the time in their second home in the Poconos. When the families get together, conversation slows down to a trickle within the first hour. When Ralph and Lois bring up remembrances of Mom and Dad, Ralph's children get restless and bored and want to know what can they do, and "when are we going to leave?" Within an hour and a half after the children's hassle, Ralph offers a weak excuse for leaving—something about avoiding the traffic going into Manhattan on a Sunday evening. Lois and her brother hug goodbye, both wishing that something more could have come from the family reunion.

John is the proprietor of a small business in the local area. He is a workaholic who skips meals and eats on the fly. He has had intermittent lower back trouble for several years. He makes complaints sporadically regarding his wife's lack of attention to his emotional needs. He admits that once he initiates the blaming remark, he is not able to shut off the automatic barrage of denigrating statements.

Several hours after the verbal barrage by her husband, Lois would slip into the kitchen and devour triple-decker sandwiches and assorted pastries. The emotional hurt always subsided following the raid on the refrigerator. However, the next morning, she would begin to knit a series of negative self-statements regarding how fat she was becoming and that she was becoming sexually undesirable. These statements would act as a brief buffer between snacks.

If she caught a reflection of herself in the mirror while window-shopping in town, or a casual remark by a friend about her weight gain, or a renewed verbal attack by her husband, these experiences would act as a stimulus to raid the refrigerator.

Dr. Tanous used his psychic gift to identify the primary emotional trauma, which led to her pattern of binge eating. He saw her as a child—a little girl coming home from school. Furthermore he described her home and the neighbourhood. Then he said: "At the age of eight you were riding your bike in your parents' neighbourhood. As you turned the corner of an intersection, you lost your balance and fell off the bike. You sustained a broken hip from the accident. During your recuperation period, your mother attempted to cover up for her guilt feelings by stating repeatedly: 'If you had some padding—extra weight around you, you would not have broken your hip.'"

Alex used his psychic insights and made additional interpretations. "Lois, during your recovery process you separated your conscious thoughts from your feelings. When you heard your mother state that you needed extra weight for protection, you translated her statement in a magical way and applied her prescription, not only for protection from future physical hurts but emotional ones as well. Thus, this protection myth had become etched in your psyche and you continued to over subscribe to it on an unconscious level whenever your inner and/or outer conflicts coincided and escalated."

He directed Lois to open her eyes. Her face was animated and her eyes were bright and clear. She had remembered the accident at age eight. Lois was astonished that Alex had been able to provide her with such details concerning the traumatic event and her conscious and unconscious maneuvers to protect herself from physical and emotional hurts.

Alex assured her that if she kept the psychic insight conscious in her daily activities, she would find "snacking and binge eating unappetizing, distasteful."

Lois began to make a number of intuitive connections into her mental and emotional states during her recovery from the broken hip. She recalled instances of feeling alone and abandoned. Both her parents worked outside the home. Their places of employment were considerable distances from the home. The family car had to suffice for basic transportation. Each working day they left home fifteen minutes before seven in order to beat the rush hour traffic around the beltway.

She recalled the morning scenario: a wet kiss and a brief hug from Mom and a pat on the head and a gentle stroke on the cheek from Dad. As they parted from the room they would say: "See you later, dear. Oh! If you get hungry there's plenty of food in the refrigerator, including your favorite snacks."

Lois recalled several fond memories of her brother's attempts to be loyal to her by staying home with her. He demonstrated his loyalty by feigning fevers and forecasting that he could sense that a cold was imminent, that last winter's virus had taken up residence in his body and never left him. Later, he would admit that the last excuse was obtained from an older boy in school. At other times, he would lay claim to unspecified body aches. When questioned closely by his parents regarding these maladies, he would unequivocally state: "She needs me. We're a team." His parents applied verbal manipulation to bring about a forced confession that he might derive some personal gain in staying home from school, such as watching TV, playing games and getting out of tests at school. Predictably, Ralph would have a pained look on his face when his hidden agenda was exposed. He discharged his angry feelings by expelling air from his nostrils several times and stomped his feet. Then he would pick up his books and brown bag lunch and proceed to the car in silence.

Ralph's dynamic role helped the family to maintain a homeostatic balance. His role as rescuer in the family counter-balanced the parents' guilt feelings. His demonstration of loyalty to his sister enabled her to lift up her mood a notch or two from feeling alone and abandoned.

Evaluation Phase

After mutual collaboration with Drs. Schwinge and Tanous, Lois agreed to pursue the following goals in treatment:

- To follow medical procedures to deal with current sinus and ear infections.
- To utilize Dr. Tanous' psychic insights to help her to limit her food intake.
- To use "thought stopping techniques" to interrupt negative self-statements.
- To encourage her husband to seek psychotherapy for himself.

Lois was instructed how to use the thought stopping technique as an emergency technique to reduce her anxiety in two areas: one, when she became aware that she was making quiet negative statements to herself and the other immediately following one of her husband's verbal harangues.

The procedure consists of three basic steps. First, Lois was instructed to say the word "stop" silently whenever she became conscious of making negative statements about herself. Her negative chain of self-statements became almost automatic whenever she became aware of her increasing anxiety while bored of being left alone in the house during the evening and consigned to watch TV reruns or predictable sit-coms. The major anxiety-producing situation followed her husband's ritual harangue. Step two of the procedure consisted of silently saying the word "relax" immediately following the word "stop." The third and final step consisted of silently making a positive statement following directly upon the word "relax." Dr. Schwinge, provided her with a list of positive self-statements, such as: "I am a worthwhile person. I can handle my anxiety in a constructive fashion without resorting to food binges."

Middle Phase

In this phase of therapy, Dr. Schwinge used free association techniques to locate early traumas in Lois' childhood, which set in motion her phobias. She asked Lois to relax and to locate herself at any age prior to the bike accident, which occurred when she was eight years old. She recalled travelling on an airplane for the first time. The stewardess announced that all passengers would "please, fasten your seat belts." Suddenly she felt trapped and fearful and began to make demands on her parents to leave the airplane immediately. She also complained that there was less air in the cabin of the plane. Her parents asked the stewardess for assistance. There were several seats unfilled in the first class section of the plane. The family moved up to that section. A compromise was struck between her parents and Lois: namely that as soon as the plane landed they would be the first ones off. Her parents gave repeated reassurances to Lois during the one hour flight. To this day, Lois is petrified of flying. The only exception was the flight to Florida at the time of her father's funeral.

In a subsequent session, while in a relaxed state, Lois made a significant discovery about herself. This time she recalled an incident when she was three years old. She was in her parents' home. She recalls that she had just rubbed the sand out of her sleepy eyes. As she looked around the dark room she spotted a small night-light. She felt that she had been left behind by her parents. Her legs felt as heavy as lead as she made her way from the bedroom, down the dark hallway to the living room. She couldn't tolerate the feeling of being left alone and so she screamed. The babysitter came running in from another room and comforted her. Lois remembers that the babysitter gave her cookies for a snack and a little glass of milk and told her it would make her feel better.

Lois provided Dr. Schwinge with additional information regarding her phobias during her high school years. In adolescence, her phobias became noticeable to others outside the family. If classmates came by and invited her for a ride around the city, she had to tell them that she found it impossible to sit in the back seat of cars because she had the feeling of being closed in. If the car trip was unavoidable she would periodically scan the position of the lock on the front door of the passenger side to see if it remained unlocked. She also avoided social gatherings, picnic areas, movie houses, class trips to nearby cities, and using elevators in department stores. Exposure to these situations triggered phobia reactions.

Dr. Schwinge led Lois into a discussion centering on her fears of cars and airplanes. Lois associated her mother's death with these fears. Her mother's dying was very hard for her to handle. She found it emotionally difficult to believe in the finality and unrepeatable experience of death. From this death experience, she believes that if she were to sit near a cemetery, she would fall in a grave.

She associated landing in an airplane like being in a coffin. Lois was afraid that she was going to fall into the coffin. Dr. Schwinge made the interpretation that the airplane, and being close to the door in order to get out, might be related to the fact that she might die. Lois made the association with an experience she had while traveling in the back of a car on Memorial Day. Her friend from the neighbourhood had died the previous week and it was customary to place flowers on the grave. Dr. Schwinge pointed out to her that when she talked about death she had a smile on her face. When Dr. Schwinge pointed out the incongruence between the words she used to refer to death and the smile on her face Lois was stunned.

Throughout the following sessions Dr. Schwinge guided Lois through the maze of obstacles surrounding her views of death. Lois admitted to some romanticized notions regarding death. However, she quickly added that she knew that these notions would not hold up to the test of reality. Lois' mother's death had taken a toll on her emotional resources. She had difficulty in finding a meaning in her dying.

Dr. Schwinge focused on the positive contributions, which her mother had made to her. Furthermore, she helped her to identify inner sources of strength.

Final Evaluation

Lois' seesaw struggle with keeping weight off is still present. At this point of writing, she is fifteen pounds over her normal body weight. The weight gain was accumulated within the past six weeks. At that point, her husband had renewed his angry verbal attacks upon her. Subsequently he would spew out a grocery list of frustrations that he had regarding the pain in his lower back, negative things concerning his job, auto traffic, etc. Lois, realizing that she was starting to accelerate her weight gain phase, asked her husband to seek out a psychiatrist for help with his problems. Currently he is engaged in therapy.

Dr. Schwinge congratulated Lois on her ability to assert herself with her husband and to take more charge of her life. Prior to entering therapy, Lois' sense of worth was centered in others and not in herself. By limiting her daily activities to familiar surroundings, she was perceived by friends as a shy and timid person.

Lois made modest gains regarding her phobic reactions. Currently she feels more comfortable when riding in a car, eating in restaurants and meeting nonaggressive people for the first time. Lois adamantly refuses to board an airplane or take an ocean cruise. She was able to use Dr. Tanous' psychic insight and profited from the self-relaxation techniques taught her by Dr. Schwinge.

CHAPTER 7

PEEK-A-BOO, I SEE YOU

~

June is a rather attractive, recently married, thirty-three year old. Within the past eighteen months she married a highly successful professional and became an instant stepmother of three children: Thomas 13, Marie 11, and Ann 8. This period of regrouping and reorganization has been stressful on each family member. The children reported that they wished that their real mother come back and that this "young witch" would leave them alone. Thomas, a gifted student, began to have academic and behavioral problems at school. His recent report card revealed four D's and one F. He has been suspended from school twice. Teachers readily admit that he challenged authority and provoked fights with other students.

Marie stayed with her father and June for three months following the wedding ceremony. June and

Marie became embroiled in conflicts; issues such as calling June mother; setting limits for study, play and bedtime. The negotiations between June and Marie were generally unsatisfactory. Immediately following each conflict, Marie would contact her mother in New Jersey and demand that a car be sent to pick her up. Mother usually complied.

Ann, the youngest, has begun to withdraw from family conversations. She retreats to the den and gives her attention to TV. Most recently she has begun to focus her attention on her fingers and engage in conversation with imaginary playmates. These playmates are usually cartoon characters.

James' profession is very demanding. Fourteen-hour days are not unusual. He is a very meticulous person who places high value on order, clear thinking, procedures and rules. The children eagerly await his return in the evenings. He withholds his affection until June reports on their conduct during the day. She feels trapped. She and the children have been struggling to establish a relationship.

If the children tested June's patience on a particular day, she would also receive James' anger while the children were sitting in the room. June would, in turn, become angry and go to the bedroom. The children would be laughing. The father would attempt to explain why he was upset with them and that they should attempt to try to be nice to June. He would knock on June's door and ask for forgiveness. Frequently, he attributed his display of temper to some upsetting events that he had at the office or the evening traffic jam. Occasionally he would simply say: "I don't know any other way to handle it." Sometimes they would acknowledge that they wished that these things wouldn't happen. At other times, June would be left alone in her room and her husband would remove himself to the guest room at the end of the hall.

In the silence of her bedroom, June began to experience a great fear of being attacked. She knew that no one was in the room. She checked the closet, under the bed, in the back of the drapes, and very gingerly peeked outside. She would then go to her husband's room, wake him up and explain what was happening to her. In the beginning he surmised that she just wanted to make up and that he should be spending more time with the family.

Her fears continued despite his effort to come home from work earlier and the fledgling promises of the children to be less testy with her. June was convinced that the old Tudor home in which they were living was the culprit of her fears. She prevailed upon her husband to purchase a very modern home with a pool and horses.

They promised to be good little people until they were a hundred years old.

A month after settling into the new home, the children's problems remained unchanged. June had an elaborate electronic system installed. She became more fearful about her being alone even during the daylight hours. She began inviting friends over to her home in order to fill up her day and thus minimize the feelings of being attacked. June has been having difficulty in sleeping and eating. Five years ago she was a fashion model and had an established pattern of being vigilant about her weight; however, she has lost her appetite. Her husband and children spend time coaxing her to eat.

Shortly after the Christmas holidays, she made an appointment to see Dr. Schwinge. She presented two problems to the psychiatrist: the fear of being attacked, and marital and family difficulties. She engaged in therapy for a ten-month period.

June arrived ten minutes early for the initial interview. She, an ex-fashion model, was tastefully dressed. Her figure was slim. June's eyes searched the psychiatrist's face for support, signs of empathy—her fears and problems where finally to be unearthed.

She began the interview with some nervousness in her voice, and related how her fear of being attacked was ruining her marriage, jeopardizing her fragile relationships with the step-children and causing her friends to refuse her invitations for afternoon and evening meetings in her home.

June became tearful when she recalled her unsuccessful attempts to deal with her fear of being attacked even after moving into the new house, installing elaborate burglar alarm systems, and manipulating friends to sit with her while her husband and children were out of the house.

Towards the end of the session she hinted that her relationship with her husband was rather rocky and that he had a high sexual interest in other women. June provided Dr. Schwinge with some basic information regarding her parents and her family life.

Family History

June is the second oldest of seven children—five girls and two boys. The births of the first five children—four girls and a boy—were spaced eighteen months apart. The remaining two boys and a girl were four and two years apart, respectively.

She describes her father as distant and cold, with very rough edges. He was frequently verbally abusive and sometimes physically abusive to his wife and the three older children. He drank to the point of intoxication, periodically, and was secretive about his trips into town in the evening. Her mother was described as a passive woman who had great difficulty in coping with her husband, children and home.

June's father was a blue-collar worker in a manufacturing mill in the South. All the children were encouraged to obtain jobs after school in order to supplement the family income. Her mother's philosophy was "make do with what you have." Her parents encouraged the children to leave the small Southern town and find opportunity in the larger industrial cities in the North. Each child took their parents advice on this point and relocated in the larger Northern cities.

At age fifteen, June won a beauty contest in her sophomore year in high school. This award boosted her spirits. From that time forward, she continued to seek employment as a model. She was moderately successful and garnered a comfortable living following high school. She had two serious relationships with men.

Dr. Schwinge introduced June to the concept of a remarriage family (REM). A REM family is created by marriage of two persons, one or both of whom have been previously married and are now divorced, separated or widowed and who may or may not have children of the previous union living in or visiting. She explained that newly formed REM families have a need to negotiate rules, establish authority guidelines, set priorities, facilitate successful mourning of the previous intact family and accept and tolerate the differences between the current REM family and the previous family.

Dr. Schwinge suggested three REM family goals that June may wish to pursue. They were:

- To consolidate the REM couple as a unit and establish their authority in the system.
- To facilitate mourning of the previous family, former partner, old neighbourhoods, friends and way of life.
- To help the family member to accept and tolerate the differences between REM and the idealized intact family.

Dr. Schwinge considered that family therapy would be useful for June and the family and recommended that family therapy be utilized concurrently with June's individual psychotherapy. June made the suggestion to her husband and children and they commenced family therapy within three weeks.

In the second session, June was visibly upset. She had seen her husband leave her side at a cocktail party and proceed to a vacant study with a recently divorced woman. Thirty minutes later, both emerged. June was furious and they had been less than civil to each other all week. She wanted to understand why her husband does these things. She briefly described his background.

James' father was a European immigrant who labored on the dock in New York harbour until his retirement five years ago. His father was absent from the home during the greater part of the day and evening hours. Wildcat strikes, ethnic squabbles and unreported beatings and knifings caused his father to carry a weapon to work on a daily basis. James and his only sister, Rita, ten years his senior, told June that their father used sarcasm and ridicule to attempt to control their self-expression. Rita landed a job with an advertising firm shortly after high school graduation and advanced to a vice-president position by the time James graduated from high school. She was confident that James would be a successful professional and thus underwrote his expenses during undergraduate and professional school. Rita provided him with a generous clothing allowance and encouraged him to make up for those financially difficult years by wearing trendy flashy clothing so that others would notice him and count him among the up and coming successful professionals.

He has since repaid his debts to his sister and is eternally grateful for her confidence and support. Rita is emotionally distant from her father. James, on the other hand, purchased a condominium for his father upon his retirement and makes repeated offers of economic assistance whenever his father would have such a need.

James and Rita agreed that their father has changed little over the years. He continues to remain sarcastic and belittles their achievements. June reports that James continues to visit his father every two months. After each visit he sugar-coats his father's remarks and simply says: "He is my father and I owe him."

June said she was tired of making excuses for her husband's behavior. She loved him but was unable to understand why he chose to relate to women with double-entendres and sexual nuances in his manner. June was sure that he loved her but needed help with his need to have sexual conquests over women.

Dr. Schwinge suggested that her husband consider individual psychotherapy. He took June's suggestion and began therapy shortly thereafter.

Evaluation Phase

During the initial evaluation phase of therapy, additional information regarding June's parents was obtained. June's family moved frequently—about every fifteen months. This uprooting had an impact on her ability to develop friendships. Her father drank to the point of intoxication several evenings per week.

June has vivid memory of her father's bedroom. He had a shoulder holster and gun, which hung over the bed's headboard. She was very fearful of even entering the bedroom. He complained rather frequently that someone was prowling outside.

She liked treats; however, when her mother would take the children to the store for candy, the father would accuse her of infidelity. Through the years, June reviewed these men who acted friendly towards her mother. She did not ever remember her mother being demonstrably affectionate with men. She occasionally wonders why her father would have made such statements.

June's goals were to:

- Develop insights and understanding regarding herself and relationships with others.
- Use relaxation techniques to reduce daily anxiety.
- Consider concurrent treatment modalities, including family therapy.
- Explore alternative means to more quickly identify early childhood traumatic memories.
- Increase self-expression.
- Become more congruent with her thoughts and feelings.

- Become more assertive.
- Claim an authority role in the family.
- Claim ownership of her behavior and feelings.
- Express her love and confidence for the children through affection and limit-setting.
- Engage in activities which will increase her self-esteem and self-confidence.
- Search for opportunities which give way to hope in the future.

Dr. Schwinge explained that she frequently uses Dr. Alex Tanous to identify, more quickly, early childhood and/or genetic traumatic memories. She said that he had been extremely useful in her work with patients in the past. June was receptive to the idea of seeing Dr. Tanous in the presence of Dr. Schwinge.

Dr. Schwinge made a clinical judgement that June possessed sufficient ego strength to sustain a psychic interpretation of her problems.

Psychic Evaluation

Dr. Schwinge introduced June to Dr. Tanous. June related to Dr. Tanous her major fear of being attacked. He offered her support and encouragement that the early childhood trauma, which precipitates her present difficulties, would be found. He briefly described how he worked and gave a rationale for his unconventional healing approach.

Dr. Tanous asked June to get comfortable in her chair and relax. She closed her eyes and started to breathe slowly according to his instructions. He began to state what he was seeing in her early life. He described the home she was living in when she was eight years of age. He even described the furniture in the rooms. He paused, and then he said: "I see you in your bedroom preparing for bed. You are wearing pyjamas. Suddenly you look at the window. You look again a second time to see if your eyes are playing tricks on you. Your father is peering in the window with an enigmatical look on his face. This is too difficult for you and you have buried it in your mind all these years." June was visibly shaken. She opened her eyes and began to relate the feelings that she had regarding her relationship with her father at that time—panic, fear of being attacked, revulsion, and confusion.

Dr. Tanous told her that the recollection of this upsetting experience would be very brief and that within a week she would lose her fear of being attacked. Towards the latter half of this session, June was much more calm and began to have greater insight about the connections of her behavior and the roots of her feelings.

Middle Phase

In the middle phase of therapy, June began to take back some of her projections regarding her husband and children. She opted out of the role of "perennial peacemaker." In the past she would have automatically responded to her husband and children in a way that she would not express her feelings and opinions directly. She felt that if she spoke of that she would just add fuel to the arguments.

June had several opportunities during the following months to increase her self-expression and become more comfortable in stating her thoughts and feelings directly. The first opportunity arose when James' ex-wife initiated a custody fight. The children were being shuttled between two homes. It was difficult for them to make the transition to the different sets of rules for each home. Quite frequently, the children attempted to manipulate June by starting their requests with "Mom let us --- ." At other times they would throw a few barbs like: "Why can't you be more like our mother?" "Do you love us as much as our mother does?"

With the help of Dr. Schwinge, June was able to re-interpret the children's requests into a framework that would enable her to speak as a responsible adult and wife of their father who loved them and wanted them to be responsible for keeping the rules in that house. She, along with their father, was open to suggestions and negotiations on some of the rules of the family.

James' ex-wife settled out of court for a rather tidy sum and he obtained custody of the children. The children were confused and sad when they heard the news. They wanted to be loyal to their mother and at the same time, they were relieved of their stressful roles as "little messengers" between former spouses. Although the roles of "go-betweens" or "message carriers" had some advantages for them, the difficulty of separating out the parents' requests from their own needs and feelings was overwhelming at times.

June was supportive of the children during this difficult period. She acknowledged their anger regarding their predicament; reiterated her love and support for them and reinforced her idea that they all would be able to get through this individually and as a family. She reflected on a statement that Dr. Schwinge used with her quite frequently: "If you have a future to hope in, your past and present difficulties can be put into perspective." As the opportunities presented themselves, June helped the children to build a future by assisting them in developing a hopeful outlook for the future.

Dr. Schwinge reminded June that it is important to buoy up the children's spirits; furthermore, she stressed that one doesn't have to give up in life just because the choices we have to make are hard.

For the past eighteen months, June had permitted her husband to weave a web of excuses and rationalizations regarding his chronic lateness. As June's self-confidence increased, she prepared herself to disentangle his web by asking him to become more responsible by phoning her when he was on his way home. This would give her the opportunity to prepare supper. In the past, suppers were eaten by her and the children. He would arrive home about fifteen minutes before their bedtime. He would apologize for his lateness, simply saying that he had grabbed a hamburger earlier. The children would ask him to extend the bedtime rule by one hour—just this time. He would suspend the rule again. June would pout and spend time knitting or on a craft project. James would watch TV for a while or go to bed.

June developed a strategy to disentangle the web. First, she told the children that they needed to be clear and forceful with their father. They had complained that they wanted to spend more time with him; however, they did not say that they needed him home. June told them that they should be very specific about their needs with their father. Then, she went to his office at the end of the day. He had seen his last client one hour ago. The secretary said that he would be returning within the hour. An hour and thirty minutes later, he returned to his office. He was surprised to see her. She told him that she was tired of sitting home with the children and that he had better begin developing a relationship with her and the children. After this meeting, James made a significant shift in the ratio of time spent with the family and his profession.

The next day he was running behind with some of his clients. He had his secretary call and give her an approximate time when he would arrive home, and if she needed him he was going to the library for a few minutes. June called the library to ask him about supper. He came to the phone and made a recommendation for the dessert. Supper and family time in the evening increased beyond a satisfactory level.

As June made progress in therapy, she listened more intently to her husband's conversations with her, the children and others. She was struck with the thought of how many times he called attention to himself and his tendency to be rude to others if they did not agree with his point of view. She began asking James to clarify his statement and encouraging him to continue the conversation with her in spite of their apparent differences of opinion.

Terminal Phase

During a session with Dr. Tanous, June remarked that his psychic insight into the origin of her anxiety of being attacked had helped to dissolve the fear almost immediately. The transmission of his psychic energy, subsequent to his psychic insight, detoxified this experience and June was able to be in a position to profit more fully from the positive growth experiences from individual psychotherapy. Dr. Schwinge remarked that June had not suffered a relapse of anxiety regarding being attacked.

During the terminal phase of therapy, June began to take more responsibility for her life. She had more energy to do some of the housework and cut the contracted housekeeping hours in half. She felt less guilty about purchasing clothing for herself.

The dominant gains, which June derived from therapy, were: freedom from the overwhelming anxiety of being attacked; more congruency with her thoughts and feelings; an increase in self-esteem and self-confidence; her husband is spending more time at home with the family.

The children continue in individual and family therapy. Thomas has made considerable academic improvement. He is experiencing his first flush with adolescence and is in need of support, love and limit setting. Marie sees her therapist with relative frequency. She has found new friends at school and has become more pleasant and cooperative around the house. Ann continues to have difficulty in accepting the divorce. She sees a child psychiatrist on a bi-weekly basis. She, a gifted child, is somewhat behind in her schoolwork but continues to be quiet and withdrawn for shorter periods of time.

CHAPTER 8

SURVIVAL FEARS
BEFORE BIRTH

~

Tom is a fifty-one year old robust Caucasian husband and father of two children who has been experiencing acute depression for the past few weeks. He has a blood pressure problem, which flares up periodically under stress. Tom smokes three packs of cigarettes per day and has difficulty refusing after dinner desserts. Also, he fears heights, being alone and being surrounded.

During the middle of December, 1981, Tom's sister, Marsha underwent open-heart surgery, which was unsuccessful. She never regained consciousness following the surgery. Since her death, Tom has found himself crying and calling in sick at work. Three days before Tom made contact with Dr. Schwinge, he became depressed when he heard that an attempt was made on the life of a political leader in a South American country. The politician had been visiting a small village at the time. Tom's nephews lived in that village and were actively aligned with the politician. The newsperson on TV reported that there were casualties. Tom assumed that his nephews were wounded or killed. He telephoned and received information that they were unharmed and in good health; however, this information did not ease his emotional problems. In fact, Tom refused to go to work and reported that he had a tingling urination frequency. Tom was referred, by his minister, to Dr. Schwinge. He told his pastor that he had a history of crying at happy occasions like weddings, and in restaurants and closed environments.

Family History

Tom's parents are deceased. They passed along a Pennsylvania Dutch formula of hard work and perseverance to equal success. He is the father of five children. Two sisters are deceased. He has a younger brother and sister who live on the East Coast.

Following his graduation from high school, Tom enlisted in the U.S. Navy. His test scores provided him with an opportunity to attend Officer Training School. He received his commission and served with the Pacific fleet for four years. Shortly before his discharge, he met Amy, who would later become his wife.

Tom and Amy have been married for thirty-two years. They have two children, Robert and John. Robert is a skilled craftsman. John is a college freshman.

For the past twenty-five years, Tom has been employed by a large manufacturing firm. His promotions have been frequent. Currently he holds a senior executive level position. This position, in his words, is filled with high stress.

Evaluation Phase

Within the first three sessions in therapy, Tom found himself calling in sick at work more frequently and having crying spells. He found himself crying at weddings. When he looked around in the reception hall, he spotted a group of senior couples seated at various tables. He began to remember experiences that he had with his parents. He remembered wanting his mother's attention while she was cooking and cleaning their home. Most especially, he remembered his attempt to persuade his mother, a schoolteacher, to stay home and skip school.

Tom entered this session in a low mood. He stated that he had been thinking about his sister these past few days. Clara and Ray had a stable marriage in his view. He enjoyed their company. Since Clara's death, Tom is afraid to call Ray because he is sure that he will break down and cry. He concludes that his crying will upset everyone.

He continued to mourn his sister Clara's death. Towards the latter half of the session, Tom brought up the topic of death. Shortly after the death of his mother, Tom felt his mother's presence on two distinct occasions. The strongest impression he had was while playing the organ in the family living room. The sense of her presence was so great that Tom stopped playing the organ and turned around, half expecting to see her. On the other occasion, he did not feel she was physically present, but that she was present in some way.

Psychic Evaluation

As Tom entered the next phase of therapy, he had to roll up his sleeves and grapple with the thorny aspect of his psychic roots.

In the beginning of the fourth session, Tom was introduced to Dr. Tanous by Dr. Schwinge. After the greetings were ex-changed, Dr. Schwinge asked Dr.

Tanous to make a psychic diagnosis of Tom's condition. Dr. Tanous turned his energy to Tom's genetic memory area. Before Dr. Tanous identified three early traumatic experiences in Tom's life, he assured him that what he was about to tell him would be useful in his recovery from his depression and fears. Alex interpreted these experiences as centrally connected to Tom's present condition. The first was Tom's dilemma prior to birth. The umbilical cord had been wrapped around his neck and he had concern for his survival outside the womb.

The second genetic memory centered on Tom's birth. Tom was born at home. The local physician was not able to make a visit to the home prior to Tom's birth. Providentially, Tom's father had been present at the birth and removed the umbilical cord from Tom's neck. This information had been substantiated later by the client's aunt.

The third genetic memory focused on Tom's contact with a corpse. When Tom was two years old, his father took him to a funeral home. As he and his father approached the coffin, Tom suddenly found himself being lifted up in his father's arms. Then his father suspended him over the corpse in the coffin. Tom was frightened and upset but did not cry.

During the last few moments of the interview, Tom indicated an interest in Dr. Tanous' psychic interpretation of his early experiences. Tom asked him how could he possibly know all the deaths in his past life. Dr. Tanous gave a very brief discussion on how his abilities were tested at the ASPR and the results of these experiments.

The efforts of a psychiatrist and psychic are directed to bring these memories to the client's awareness in order to give him/her the opportunity to enhance their autonomy and freedom from fear.

These memories are not necessarily limited to experiences outside the womb. Clients carry memories of the womb experience. They also carry memories of parents', grandparents', or ancestors' fears and unresolved problems. Just as our parents and grandparents pass on their genetic strengths as unusual abilities and their weakness as the potential of genetic diseases, they also pass on an inheritance of their experiences in the genetic memory.

At the end of the evaluation period Tom agreed to pursue the following goals:

- Comply with medical regimen to lift his depression.
- Reduce cigarette intake by ½ pack a day.
- Reduce blood pressure by using self-hypnotic techniques.
- Return to normal weekly work schedule.

- Resolve incomplete mourning for family members.

Dr. Schwinge had prescribed medication to help relieve the depression. There was a hiatus between therapy sessions during the Christmas holidays. Tom regressed somewhat. He felt his sister's loss most acutely. Her birthday and wedding anniversary occurred during the holidays. Tom had started to experience headaches, dizziness, and his blood pressure climbed. In order to bring his blood pressure under control, his physician prescribed additional medication. Dr. Schwinge helped Tom to relax and recall his childhood. Tom was allowed to choose a happy age. He chose five years of age. In the trance state, he described a farmhouse with high ceilings and cold floors. His mother prepared delicious meals and baked pies and cakes quite frequently. His brothers and sisters would chase him around. He received a lot of cuddling from his mother.

Dr. Schwinge introduced the scene of a boy skipping a rock across a lake. She asked Tom if he thought it were a peaceful scene. He replied that it was. Suddenly tears began to form at corners of his eyelids. He expressed apprehension about his problems as a child and being a mature man and controlling himself.

Middle Phase

Tom reported that the prescribed medication was of some benefit; however, his work attendance remained spotty. Dr. Schwinge set up a series of suggestions designed to help Tom to disrupt his depressing thoughts. She gave Tom various homework assignments—such as counting his negative thoughts, identifying the consequences of his thought—and looking at some of the assumptions proved helpful to Tom. It gave him an opportunity to experience a modicum of control over his negative thoughts.

He made a valiant effort to reduce his cigarette consumption and succeeded in limiting his habit to fewer than ten cigarettes a day. Tom was very proud of this accomplishment.

The office work was more difficult for Tom in this phase of therapy. A six-week business slump had his co-workers on edge and in each other's hair. His boss made increased demands upon Tom. His blood pressure spiked several times. Tom called in sick a number of times. Memories of his departed family members became more prominent in his private reflections.

Dr. Schwinge guided Tom into the area of grief. She encouraged Tom to express these painful feelings of loss, which had attached themselves to memories of his family. These painful memories, she said, would heal in time and when the healing is complete Tom would have the courage to reinvest emotionally in others.

In one particular session the psychiatrist used an empty chair as a prop in order to get Tom in touch with unspoken feelings about not being able to say goodbye to Clara. Tom was embarrassed to admit that he felt angry that his sister had left him. The doctor asked him to imagine Clara present in the empty chair. What would you say to her? The question had a calming effect. Tom was able to let out a stream of associations about his sister, the good times in childhood, the silly fights, missed opportunities to be closer, and the guilt about how things could have been better. This was the first time that Tom had opened up about the feelings he had for his sister. Dr. Schwinge outlined the various phases in the grief process. She stated that in order for the healing of grief to be complete, one needs to establish new relationships and affirm the goodness of life. Tom was instructed to continue to be loyal to his departed family members by using the good memories of them to share hope with others that it is possible to live and feel good about life and people again.

Dr. Schwinge began to make timed interpretations regarding the psychic insights into the pre-birth experience and early childhood experiences and Tom's current conflicts. Dr. Tanous made the interpretation that Tom has over-emphasized the aspects of uncertainty regarding survival after birth. This has been a prevailing theme in his dealing with adverse situations. Dr. Schwinge stated that it is curious that Tom does not view his father's removal of the umbilical cord as a providential call to life. Tom, a practicing Christian, gave intellectual assent to the existence of a hereafter, but actively maintained an ambivalence when the subject was introduced in social gatherings. He was encouraged to discuss his views on the hereafter, as well as his experiences of God in his life, with the local pastor.

At the beginning of each session Tom was instructed to give a weekly account of positive feelings associated with assertive statements and completed tasks. The psychiatrist focused on developing interventions, which would help him to follow through with workable tasks in order to achieve reachable goals. He was able to re-interpret his boss' angry, caustic and guilt-inducing remarks as the boss' way of attempting to handle what was going on inside himself. The boss had been dubbed, "the walking volcano", by the co-workers. These interventions proved helpful. No longer did Tom hold himself responsible for his boss' problems.

Final Evaluation

Tom had been able to work through much of his active grieving over family members. He showed hopeful signs by picking up a renewed interest in his wife and children. His smoking habit is being held to five cigarettes per day. At his place of employment, Tom is working a full schedule of hours and reports the stress level is tolerable. He has more confidence in living and can say "no" to his anxiety more effectively. The noxious effects of the genetic and childhood memories have been somewhat neutralized. Whenever Tom is asked to assume a supine position and close his eyes in the dentist chair, he has a heightened sense of being in an open casket; however, he has had very good success in not escalating his anxiety to the point of incapacity during the experience. The anti-depressant medication has been discontinued. Currently he is still being maintained on blood pressure medication.

CHAPTER 9

THE SECOND SIN

~

Mildred is a thirty-four year old Caucasian married woman and the mother of a baby girl, but she had never received the kind of training and support needed to grow into an independent adult. Her parents' "sin" had been to let her feel dependent, helpless and guilty in the bad situations in their family life as she was growing up.

She had been in therapy on two previous occasions before entering into therapy with Dr. Schwinge in September of 1981. The previous experiences were limited to a few sessions and centered on current crises. One was precipitated by an abortion some ten years ago. The other was a most recent attempt on her own life.

In the spring of 1981, she was admitted to a psychiatric unit in a general hospital following her attempt on her own life by slashing both wrists. Upon admission, her chief complaints were: that she couldn't feel anything when relating to her parents or her husband, had a great deal of pain in her head, suffered from insomnia, had a decreased appetite, and a lack of interest in life.

She was in the second trimester of her pregnancy. It was her intention to bring the child to full term and move in with her mother and stepfather until the child was a few months old.

Mildred was discharged from the psychiatric unit within ten days of admission. She lived with her parents until several weeks after the birth of her healthy baby girl.

Family History

Mildred was born in a small mining village in northeastern Pennsylvania. She describes her neighbourhood as "out at the elbows." During the first three years of her life, she lived with her parents and maternal grandparents. Her earliest memories at this age were loud, boisterous arguments and yelling by her parents and grandparents. Mildred's paternal grandparents, her father and his two brothers and sister were alcoholics. Shortly after her third birthday, she and her parents moved to a small suburb in Allentown. Her father was a construction worker. This occupation necessitated his being punctuated with predictable uprooting.

A few weeks before kindergarten opened its doors for the fall semester, Mildred had a tonsillectomy, and developed a bout of rheumatic fever. When the rheumatic fever abated, she began to stutter. This condition remained relatively unchanged until her senior year in high school. Mildred did not receive speech therapy for her condition and she did not suffer any complications from the rheumatic fever.

At age eight, Mildred's mother ordered her husband, Bob, out of the house. He had been abusing alcohol for the length of the marriage. He had provided a modest income for his wife and family. Although he was not physically abusive, her mother had made repeated attempts to translate her father's attitude, behavior and motives in the worst possible light.

When the divorce became final, Bob continued to visit Mildred on a bi-monthly basis until she was twelve. Their time together consisted of visits to the park, movies, and treats at McDonalds. Eventually the conversations became knotted with clichés and long silences. Mildred had bought into mother's plan for dissolving the emotional relationship of Bob and the family. She felt guilty about her part in her mother's plan. She felt especially guilty when she knew that her silence would lead her father to conclude that she wasn't having a good time with him on a particular visit. He would ask her what she was feeling and she would get anxious. Mildred knew that she wanted to be loyal to her mother and yet she felt something for Dad also. The moment she would open her mouth she began to stutter. Bob was sympathetic. Sometimes he would blame himself for making her nervous.

Bob's surname rhymed very easily with many words. Mildred became the object of ridicule by callous classmates who would taunt her on her way home from school. She became upset and her stuttering would increase greatly. She longed to tell her Dad about the mean classmates. However, he lived a hundred miles away, and she knew that Dad could not be available when she needed his protection to put those kids straight. Mildred tucked these feelings in the back of her memory, thereby removing a potential opportunity for the father to help her. The father and daughter visits began to get shorter. Somewhere in the middle of seventh grade, her Dad terminated the visits. He would resume the visits a few years later.

Seven years after the divorce, Mildred's mother, Bernie entered a second marriage, with Walter, a short, middle-aged businessman. He was sixteen years Bernie's senior. Walter was a very kind, soft-spoken gentleman with gray sideburns and with a moderate paunch. This was quite in contrast to Bob, a blue-eyed blond, who was a rugged-looking construction worker and an action-oriented person.

Mildred graduated from high school and obtained an associate degree from a community college in midstate. Her first job after graduation was as assistant manager in a small apothecary. With five years of managerial experience under her, she joined her stepfather's company. Mildred worked her way up in the company to vice-president. Her apprenticeship consisted of demonstrating competency in various departments of the company.

High school was particularly painful to Mildred during freshman and sophomore years. Her stuttering continued, although it had decreased considerably from the early onset. She had a severe case of acne and was somewhat plump. In her junior year she shed her excess weight. Frequently, her stuttering was hardly noticeable. She attributes the changes in herself to her first love. She described him as a serious young man who was very attentive to her and, on occasion, had a dry sense of humor. He gave her up shortly after graduation. He went off to pursue a course of studies in chemical engineering at a local university. They wrote occasionally. During the Christmas holiday they dated, but things were not the same. He started to date a girl on campus. When Mildred heard that he was dating, she went into a depression for two weeks. She was not able to work, slept little, lost her appetite and was quite tearful.

She didn't date for six months. Her girlfriend, Florence, kept bugging her to date. She introduced Mildred to Terrance. Terrance's attitude was cocky and arrogant. He walked with a swagger. Mildred and her mother did not appreciate Terrance's attitude. Throughout the course of their dating, his conversations were peppered with belittling remarks. When she indirectly confronted him with his attitude towards her, he would simply say: "I find it difficult to say sentimental stuff and so when I feel sentimental I say little rough remarks just to get your attention." Mildred settled for his explanation.

Terrance justified his rough and tough attitude to Mildred's mother by appealing to its usefulness in getting him through the Vietnam War. He promised to work on his attitude in time. Her mother was not taken in by his promise to change, however, she did not want to block her daughter's chance at marriage.

Terrance described his Vietnam experiences as horrendous. He and his company were part of a larger group, which was assigned the task of search and destroy missions. At the end of a fighting day, he would attempt to blot out the screams of his wounded comrades and sights of mangled bodies by ingesting large quantities of alcohol. The next morning he and his team were lifted by choppers and transported to the general area where they had been the day before. As they neared the area, they were greeted by V.C. gunfire. Their mission was to hurt "Charlie", repel him, secure the area, load the hurt, wounded and the dead Americans on choppers, and then return to camp. If they didn't have duty that particular evening, they would drink themselves into a deep sleep. The problem of alcohol abuse had been an established pattern prior to his discharge from the United States Army.

Terrance received an honorable discharge from the U.S. Army. Shortly thereafter, he obtained a position in the sales department of a textile company. He was promoted twice within the first sixteen months of his hiring. He was considered as a "no-nonsense, aggressive person" with his peers and demonstrated the "velvet touch" with clients during the closure phase of a contract.

Marriage

Marital discord was the predominant feature of their relationship. Their negotiation skills were poor. Terrance would proclaim that he was the head of the house and adopted a "might makes right" attitude when issues were discussed. The negotiations would be extremely brief. Mildred would bite her tongue and become quiet. Occasionally, her cheeks would become puffed but the words got stuck in her throat. Mildred would attempt to control her husband by pretending to hear only part of his demands and ultimatums. Neither she nor her husband had any goals as a couple. Individually their goals were to be calmer, to avoid fighting and to save a little money.

About ten years ago, when Mildred found out that she was pregnant for the first time, it was not planned. When she told her husband the news, he threw a temper tantrum and ordered her to have an abortion. She wanted a child but was afraid to disobey him.

After the abortion was performed, Mildred found her mood was low. She was uncomfortable with the choice, which had been foisted on her by her husband. Within a few months she started to reach out to her husband and began to place some emotional needs on him. He maintained a peripheral relationship with her by being out with the boys two nights per week and spending two nights a week working with clients in order to get more business for the company. On weekends, he would suggest visiting relatives and friends. Their time alone was reduced to a minimum.

Mildred began to sink into a depression. Her mother responded to her daughter's condition. She confronted Terrance with his neglect. He said that he didn't know what to do about her being depressed. Terrance took her to the family physician. An antidepressant was prescribed. Within six weeks Mildred's low mood had lifted somewhat. Terrance had been spending more time with her in the evenings.

Within eighteen months, Mildred and Terrance had reverted back to their old patterns. The relationship limped along for several years. It became fragile when Mildred became pregnant for the second time. This pregnancy, like the first, had been consciously unplanned.

When Mildred was three months pregnant, her husband came forward with the information that he was seeing an old girlfriend. Mildred was in shock. She slumped in her chair. Her jaw hung open. He went on to explain that this was the same woman who sent him a "Dear John" letter when he was in Vietnam. Terrance denied any sexual involvement with this woman. He did admit to dating her on a weekly basis for the past five months. He stated that he still felt something for her. Mildred became extremely upset.

Within a week, Mildred slipped into a deep depression, which was characterized by shaking, depersonalization of feeling, (unable to feel), outbursts of tears, loss of weight and an inability to sleep. Early one Sunday morning she opened a drawer in her kitchen and used a steak knife to cut her wrists. Her husband heard her scream and he quickly applied tourniquets and called the police emergency number. She was admitted to the psychiatric unit of a general hospital.

Following her discharge from the hospital, she went to live with her mother and stepfather. The baby was a healthy girl. Mildred decided to have an unofficial trial separation from Terrance.

He brought gifts for the baby and flowers for Mildred. She remained adamant in her decision to live with her mother until the child was three months old. Mildred made another decision. She decided to get into therapy with a psychiatrist. Her physician showed her a list of providers in the area. She also consulted with her friends. She chose to enter therapy with Dr. Schwinge.

Initial Evaluation

During the initial evaluation phase, Mildred presented a picture of a person who has been chronically depressed. Marital strife had extended itself throughout the entire length of the relationship. Her current physical problems include episodic headaches in the right frontal and supraorbital areas, which were, most likely, caused by stress/sinus related and a mild eosinophilia (type of blood disorder). She also has allergies from dust, trees, grass, tobacco, chocolate, wool and cocoa.

Dr. Schwinge prescribed an antidepressant to lift her mood. This was the same medication previously prescribed by her physician following her suicide attempt.

At the end of the evaluation period, Dr. Schwinge explored with Mildred her attitude toward unconventional healers. Mildred had received a basic religious education and had a general belief in life hereafter and God's power to intervene in people's lives. She was open to the idea of having Dr. Tanous make a psychic diagnosis of her condition. Dr. Schwinge explained the basic concepts of psi in psychotherapy, its rationale and a brief description of Dr. Tanous' method of diagnosing problems.

Dr. Schwinge introduced Dr. Tanous to Mildred. Alex spent a considerable period of time in an altered-state discerning the various types of information, which he was receiving from his psychic channels. Alex reported that her energy lines in her aura were hectic and pulsated in an erratic fashion. Two numbers, 2 and 7, came through on his clairvoyant channel. These numbers were later identified with incidents in Mildred's early childhood. Alex had a vision of her at age two. She was sitting on the kitchen floor. She appeared very anxious and scanned the kitchen in search of her parents. He sensed that she had the experience of a separation anxiety. She waddled to the dining room and then into the parlor. Later she let out a scream. Her parents didn't respond. Mildred felt separated from her parents.

Dr. Tanous used the same procedures to identify a similar traumatic incident, which had occurred in Mildred's life at age seven. He saw a psychic scene in which Mildred was asking her parents questions about where she would live when she grew up. Her father and mother both agreed that she would grow up into a beautiful lady and marry a handsome man. Most probably she would move far away and not come back to visit them. Mildred was terrified at the thought of being separated from her parents. She protested and said that she didn't want to grow up. Her parents laughed. Mildred translated their laughter as a rejection of her. She was amazed that Alex was able to describe these events with such great detail. She also found Dr. Tanous' psychic interpretations interesting and enlightening. She was able to make some basic connections between past and present difficulties.

It was Dr. Schwinge and Dr. Tanous' concept that Mildred's struggle for freedom and autonomy was centered on the ingrained pattern of an anxiety of separation from her parents. They concluded that this was the core of her problems. This same pattern was being maintained in her marital relationship with Terrance. Separation anxiety was triggered environmentally whenever she felt alone and neglected by her husband. Depression quickly followed the anxiety. By then, she lacked the energy to exercise her freedom of choice to assert herself as an independent person.

The goals, which Mildred contracted to pursue during therapy, were:

- To follow medical regime to control her physical problems.
- To maintain herself on antidepressant and anti-anxiety medication.
- To practice self-hypnosis in order to reduce the frequency of anxiety headaches.
- To utilize psychic insights to help her to deal with her separation anxiety.
- To become more assertive in her relationship with her husband.
- To reduce stress by participating in behavior modifying techniques.
- To identify three positive qualities in herself.
- To look for hopeful signs in herself, her family and environment.

- To increase self-expression.
- To become more congruent with her thoughts and feelings.
- To engage in one pleasurable activity per day.
- To resume her part-time job in the community.

Middle Phase

By the eleventh session, Mildred had shown some noticeable signs of improvement in her mood. She was being maintained on her antidepressant medication. She reported positive steps in voicing her opinion, to her husband, concerning household management. She was returning to part-time employment, negotiating a babysitting schedule with her mother-in-law, improving her personal appearance, participating in a few recreational activities, such as walking in the park, going to dinner in a restaurant and enjoying conversation with co-workers in the factory. Mildred's headaches had not abated significantly. She has continued the course of treatment to control her allergies, which also contribute to the headaches. Dr. Schwinge guided Mildred into the central area of work during this phase of therapy. Mildred's task was to grapple with the sharp and biting edges of the separation anxiety experiences in her childhood and to make a resolve to successfully overcome their noxious effects in order to promote her freedom and autonomy in current relationships with family members and others.

During the following weeks Mildred had two very brief experiences with depression. The first seemed to be environmentally induced as it occurred when her boss became angry about the quality of her sewing work. The second happened when she had a flashback regarding her husband's dating his old girlfriend. Both depressions were limited to three days each.

Shortly after these incidents, Dr. Schwinge reaffirmed Mildred's worth and the nobility of her struggle. She encouraged Mildred to translate these setbacks as symptoms of freedom and autonomy. Furthermore, she pointed out that Mildred's recent depressions had lifted within a few days and that she was able to resume a normal level of functioning.

Mildred began to utilize Dr. Tanous' psychic insights into her emotional problems. For example, she became aware of the rise in her anxiety and fear whenever she was contemplating a confrontation with her husband regarding his fair share of parenting, etc. Her thoughts would lead her to the inevitable conclusion: "If I confront him, he will leave and I will be alone." With Dr. Schwinge's assistance, Mildred was able to break the heretofore automatic chain of thoughts leading to depression. Dr. Schwinge directed her to apply thought-stopping techniques to break the links in her automatic chain of thoughts. Furthermore, Dr. Schwinge stated that "the task for children is to grow and go." Mildred's parents were unable to help her to assert herself and increase her opportunities for self-confidence and self-expression. Their messages seemed to be that independent expressions are signs of disloyalty, and disloyal persons cannot be given love.

Gradually, over the next few months, Mildred, with Dr. Schwinge's guidance, began to dissolve the frozen perception she had of her parents. She took back her projections of them and began to see them as a couple, with limitations, who had struggled to obtain her love and loyalty by numerous manoeuvres which, for the most part, they were double-binding. Mildred made symbolic reconciliation gestures in therapy sessions in order to balance her relationship with the parents. Mildred began to make gains in her independence from her interjected parents. Simultaneously, Terrance began to increase his negative statements towards her.

As a fledgling independent person, Mildred was more comfortable in stating her opinion and negotiating with her husband. However, she began to have insights into his limitations, his temper tantrums, ultimatums, impulsive actions, and need to be first, right and ultimately to control. She asked Dr. Schwinge how to approach the subject of therapy for her husband. Dr. Schwinge suggested that she might offer the following statement as an inducement:

> "In order to understand me better, it may be worth your time to come in and discuss some of the difficulties you are having with me."

Terrance agreed to come in and talk with Dr. Schwinge. Terrance is currently engaged in therapy with the psychiatrist.

Final Phase

In the third phase of therapy, Mildred was able to apply relaxation techniques for relief of her headache in Dr. Schwinge's office. She reported substantial relief following her awakening from the relaxed state. However, she was unable to utilize self-relaxation techniques for headache relief at her job in the factory or in her home.

She had been promoted to a supervisory position in the factory and has gained more confidence and competence in operating various machines. Co-workers are still friendly and cooperative. Their attitudes surprised Mildred. She had thought that they would have become aloof when she was promoted to the supervising position.

Terrance reports that things are going well in the family. He is planning to renovate the home. His relationship with Mildred has improved significantly.

Mildred requested to see Dr. Tanous for a special consultation. He was impressed with the gains she had made. She told him that she was eight weeks pregnant and wanted to know the sex of the future child. He said it would be a boy. She was extremely happy for she knew that her husband had longed for a son, and she was happy that her daughter would have a baby brother. Both Dr. Tanous and Dr. Schwinge celebrated Mildred's progress.

The twenty-eighth session was the final session. Dr. Schwinge summarized Mildred's gains and asked her to specify some of her future goals and plans for her and her husband beyond the therapy experience. Mildred thanked Dr. Schwinge for her assistance in helping her to experience greater freedom and autonomy and asked her to convey the same message to Dr. Tanous.

Some months later, Mildred called to say that they had a baby boy weighing 8lbs. 9 oz. Alex was correct about the sex of the child.

CHAPTER 10

POSTSCRIPT

~

The door to the second millennium is but fifteen years away. It is our hope that greater support will be expended towards utilizing authentic psychics with demonstrated healing abilities in conjunction with mental health professionals to assist in bringing relief to individuals who suffer physically and emotionally.

Our scientific knowledge has made exponential leaps within the past decade. For example, new basic textbooks in the chemical and electronic engineering fields are being updated every thirteen months and sixteen months respectively in order to keep up with advancements in these fields.

Advances in scientific knowledge have led theoretical physicists to form new concepts of some of their basic assumptions about what constitutes reality. It behoves theoretical advisors of human development to shed nineteenth century mechanistic models of causality and adopt a theoretical framework, which will allow for additional factors such as telepathy, psychic healing, and psychic insight to play a factor in our understanding of how humans change.

If psi in psychotherapy is to take its place as a viable alternative approach in the healing of one's psyche, it needs to be tested on a large scale under strict scientific controls.

We are hopeful that future collaborative efforts among psychics, psychotherapists and researchers will yield promising therapeutic avenues for mental health. Psi in psychotherapy needs to demonstrate that it is effective and satisfying for its consumers.

In his books, *Beyond Coincidence* and *Is Your Child Psychic?*, Dr. Tanous specifies the various criteria to be utilized in assessing the authenticity of a psychic: basic pre-requisites required for candidacy, tasks, goals and struggles involved in acquiring these psychic gifts, the contraindications for continuance in the path to psychic mastery and the maladaptive uses of psychic gifts.

If, indeed, psychotherapists can utilize, in their practice, authentic psychics or themselves acquire a modicum of psychic gifts, the ultimate empirical questions need to be answered regarding psi in psychotherapy—"What kind of problems, with what type of treatment, by whom, with what level of experience, with what kind of gains and for how long?"

The more data that becomes available from answering the empirical questions, the better able we will be to assess the usefulness of psi in psychotherapy with mental health problems. Our short book represents a small step in the march for progress of psi in psychotherapy. We are hopeful that psychics, psychotherapists, researchers and those interested in parapsychology will be encouraged to make similar contributions to the field.

PSI IN PSYCHOTHERAPY

AFTERWORD

~

I can imagine that the reader will have arrived here at the end of the book in a state of mind somewhat perplexed by unanswered questions. Are psychic abilities so proven that a psychic can work productively together with a psychiatrist and psychotherapist? It may also be thought that following Alex Tanous' death in 1990, we know a lot more about the phenomena and that many of the revelations made here will no longer be relevant to our present time. I would, nevertheless, assert that there is something valuable in the text here because it is almost unique as well as timeless.

Tanous was an apparent gifted healer but also an academic who was keen not only to have his skills both scientifically tested but also applied to helping the wellbeing of others. His work has left a legacy both in the form of this previously unpublished manuscript concerning the clinical applications of his gift and, additionally, in the form of the documentation of his participation in research projects. Instances of psychic claimants actually seeking out and encouraging the latter are rare, but it means the readers who wish to check on the authenticity of Tanous' claims—and some of them are such as his control over his out-of-body-experiences, ESP and healing—may do so. However, they seem rather extraordinary upon further reading. If you are skeptically inclined or just curious, it means that you can go directly to the research reports and draw your own conclusions. A good place to begin is the summary article/biography by Callum E. Cooper (2015), but there are even recordings of some of the tests carried out on Alex Tanous at the American Society for Psychical Research, which are now available on YouTube.

How relevant is this book to modern psychotherapy? The book refers to the strict procedure or even protocol that Alex Tanous followed in working with psychiatrist Elaine Schwinge and psychotherapist Andrew Bambrick. This procedure enabled the co-operation of seemingly unlikely partners to be productive and to occur without any encroachment on each other's professional area of expertise. Today, rather than following Freudian or Jungian theories that are adhered to here in the book, most psychotherapists are eclectic in the sense of using what works for particular patients. It is fundamental to provide what research has shown to be the *universal conditions for change*: empathy, acceptance and genuineness in relating to the patient. Another important finding is that, depending on the level of these conditions, the ensuing change can be negative as well as positive. Some caregivers may then, if they are cold, demeaning and arrogant, actually make their patients more ill.

Adding to these basic conditions for change are the *therapeutic techniques* such as those of the systematic approach called cognitive behavior therapy, which defines and deals with specific problem areas one at a time. (This approach is well known in the U.S.A. through the media psychologist, Dr. Phil). Recently this has been complemented with meditative practices such as mindfulness. Some knowledge of the major theoretical contributions to psychotherapy (such as Jung and Freud) and of diagnostic formulations (such as DSM-V) may, of course, facilitate treatment. Naturally, the latter is the professional focus of the psychiatrist and psychotherapist in their contributions to the text of this book. The main author, Alex Tanous, as the psychic healer in the three-part alliance, does make it clear that it is the Jungian concept of higher states of consciousness that he feels most comfortable with. This Jungian idea of the collective unconscious does form a point of rapprochement with the current interest, ironically foremost amongst cognitive behavioral therapists, in promoting "mindfulness" amongst patients. Mindfulness can be regarded as a meditative means of creating openness to the unconscious.

The authors use some terms here that can be confusing to the reader who is familiar with those now approved by modern cognitive psychology. They refer to *genetic memory* and/or *experiences*, by which they mean a "repository of experiences from the birth of consciousness." The current term for this would be "episodic memories." The terms *genetic memory* and *genetic experiences* are, unfortunately, easily confused with genetic predispositions and vulnerabilities such as the proneness to psychotic experiences. Naturally it is important, as the authors emphasize, to know about such aspects in order to fully understand the patient's experiences.

As for the modern role of the therapist, some therapists, especially those following the tradition of the eminent psychotherapist, Carl Rogers, never actually claim to cure patients but rather to provide a relationship, within which the patients or clients can cure themselves. The psychotherapist Charles Devonshire, who was educated by Rogers, once expressed this to me in more pragmatic terms: His job was to help people who were screwed-up, to become a little looser, and those whose screws were loose, to tighten up.

Tanous saw his role as more than this. Nevertheless he does not attribute himself as the true agency of healing. In describing the role of the psychic in working with psychotherapy, he writes: "Higher consciousness is spirituality and the power that lives within us is universal ... the healing is not from me, the psychic, but rather it is because I am attuned to the consciousness of the Universe, to the heart and mind of God, and that lets the power flow through me and healing takes place."

Others, less religiously inclined, might prefer—as is often stated—to see the role as one of enabling the patient to activate his/her own internal healer and healing potential to change body and mind. There is now the established field of *psychoneuroimmunology*, which details how stress and other psychological factors facilitate positive, as well as negative, changes in the immune system. As a consequence, these changes can promote healing and promote illness.

Of course it is impossible to know how many of Tanous' cures were due to expectancy—that is what is called the placebo effect. It may, however, be more constructive to see the placebo as a positive and extensive force to be engaged in the treatment. Indeed, conscious-ness researcher, Charley Tart, prefers the term *Psychological Empowerment Practice*, appropriately shortened to PEP, instead of placebo. The physician Larry Dossey (2016) believes it is high-time time to revolutionize medical science by adding a much wider concept of placebo: one which takes into account research concerning ESP and non-local consciousness. By non-local conscious-ness, Dossey is referring to the basic connectedness in the universe indicated by some of the non-local syn-chronicities occurring in quantum physics and even now being found in biology. (It is, of course, still hotly debated whether consciousness is part of these phenomena.) For this purpose, Dossey introduces the term "telecebo" to describe the type of placebo effect that involves "an ex-teriorization of the intentions, thoughts, or emotions of a clinician toward a patient." Dossey alerts us to how, in likeness to that of psychotherapy, this effect can be posi-tive or negative depending on the clinician. Anyone who wishes to look further into these issues and is interested in how negative phenomena such as "poltergeist posses-sion" can happen and be explained, is recommended to read the theory of Walter von Lucadou (2017), a theory that builds on the above concepts.

The question still remains as to how much of the working relationship with a psychic healer, described in detail here, is accepted by contemporary psychiatry and clinical psychology? Tanous was most active during the 1970s, a cultural period in history, in which there was a greater openness to psychic experiences than is the case today. The openness stretched not only to the collaboration detailed in this book, but even to the academic world, so much so that Tanous was, for a time, engaged in giving courses at an established university about his experiences. This would not be possible today and it would entail great professional risks for psychiatrists and licensed psychotherapists to work with psychics in this way even if the latter, as was the case with Tanous, had a professional education. Research opportunities in this area are also much more limited in terms of funding.

There is, nevertheless, a contemporary interest in the clinical significance of psychic experiences and their relationship to various psychotic and dissociated states. Much of the evidence points to how these experiences are not only common and normal, but are perceived by the individuals concerned as enhancing their meaning in life. Nevertheless there exists a group of pre-psychotic individuals in which so-called "ideas of reference" and grandiose or paranoid delusions of being influenced by telepathy are present as part of disorganized thought processes. A thumb rule is that, at least in most cultures, it is not unusual to experience reading someone's mind, but believing that others are starting to read yours is not a good sign. The same is true for God: Many people report talking to God, but when God talks back, then this is a sign that you may need professional help.

Such issues, and many others of similar concern, formed the basis for a conference on the topic of "clinical parapsychology" with the papers now available in book form (Kramer, Bauer, & Hövelmann, 2012). An undue focus on pathology and symptoms has traditionally formed a part of psychiatric diagnosis but the neglect of the above normal experiences and of the many cultural differences relating to spiritual experiences, has led to the inflation and misuse of psychiatric diagnosis. As a consequence, although the latest psychiatric diagnostic manual gives some concession to cultural differences, it is still subject to serious criticism (Cassels, 2018).

A more sophisticated way of dealing with what is normal and what is potentially psychotic is to consider the degree to which the experiences are integrated into the person, versus how overwhelming they are becoming. The concept of splitting or *dissociation* becomes then highly relevant to understanding how the person deals with what may be a predisposition towards these psychic, exceptional, or anomalous experiences (Krippner & Powers, 1997).

In psychiatry there is also, at last, some recognition of the need to show respect to the individual's spiritual experiences rather than readily to diagnose them. There exists in the U.K. amongst psychiatrists a special interest group for "Spirituality and Psychiatry," which recently, under the aegis of the Royal College of Psychiatrists (2013), issued a position statement that is close to the main message of this book. The major policy change is that: "Psychiatrists, whatever their personal beliefs, should be willing to work with leaders/members of faith communities, chaplains and pastoral workers in support of the well-being of their patients, and should encourage all colleagues in mental health work to do likewise." Although I have been unable to find a similar policy statement for the American Psychiatric Association, exactly the same statement as the above is reproduced as part of the World Psychiatric Association's policy (Moreida-Ameida et al., 2016).

There are many research findings suggesting that spirituality operates by creating meaning in life, which offers a protective function against somatic illness. Despite this, the Christian Church has generally regarded the paranormal as a pagan threat or even works of the devil and finds unlikely bedfellows in the militant skeptics whereas, in fact, anomalous experiences should be seen as evidence of the various forms of spirituality (Kripal, 2014). More constructive approaches clearly are needed here. One such approach is found in the Anglican Church, which has a *Churches' Fellowship for Psychical and Spiritual Studies.* While not denying that there are those who need professional help, this approach generally regards seemingly "paranormal" claims as objective evidence of spirituality.

What can one take away from this book? It is important to choose your therapist—irrespective of whether the person is a psychiatrist, psychologist, or psychic—carefully from their track record. Tanous clearly had a good one.

Adrian Parker, Ph.D.,
University of Gothenburg, Sweden.
June, 2018

References

Cassels, C. (2018). DSM-5 Officially Launched, but Controversy Persists. *Medscape Medical News*, January 25, 2018 https://www.medscape.com/resource/dsm-5 Retrieved: 06/06/2018.

Cooper, C.E. (2015). 'Alex Tanous'. *Psi Encyclopedia.* https://psi-encyclopedia.spr.ac.uk/articles/alex-tanous Retrieved 06/06/2018.

Dossey, L. (2016) Telecebo: Beyond placebo to an expanded concept of healing. *Explore, 12,* 1-12.

Kramer, W.H., Bauer, E., & Hövelmann, G.H. (Eds.). (2012). *Perspectives of clinical parapsychology.* Bunnik, Germany: Stichting Het Johan Borgman Fonds.

Kripal, J. (2014). *Religion and the paranormal.* Chicago, U.S.A.: University of Chicago Press.

Krippner, S. & Powers, S. M. (1997). *Broken images, broken selves: Dissociative narratives in clinical practice.* Washington, DC, U.S.A.: Brunner/Mazel.

Moreira-Almeida, A., Sharma, A., van Rensburg, B.J., Verhagen, P., & Cook, C. H. (2016). WPA position statement on spirituality and religion in psychiatry. *World Psychiatry, 15* (1), 87-88. https://www.ncbi.nlm.nih.gov/pmc/articles/PMC4780301/ Retrieved: 29/06/2018.

Royal College of Psychiatrists (2013). Recommendations for psychiatrists on spirituality and religion Position Statement. https://www.rcpsych.ac.uk/workinpsychiatry/specialinterestgroups/spirituality/publicationsarchive.aspx Retrieved: 06/06/2018.

van Lucadou, W. (2017). Clinical parapsychology. *Parapsykologiske Notiser, 84,* 57-63.

CONTRIBUTOR
BIOGRAPHIES
~

Callum E. Cooper, Ph.D., is a lecturer and researcher based at the University of Northampton, U.K. He is a long-time member of the university's research group Exceptional Experiences and Consciousness Studies, and also a long-time member of the Society for Psychical Research and is a council member of the society. He is a Chartered Member of the British Psychological Society, a Professional Member of the Parapsychological Association and a Research Affiliate of Hope Studies Central, University of Alberta. He has several dozen scientific research papers and articles to his name, and has authored and edited four books to date with focus on parapsychology. He is the recipient of the Eileen J. Garrett Scholarship

(2009), the Dr. Gertrude Schmeidler Award (2014), and has received the Alex Tanous Scholarship Award several times over. In 2018, he was nominated for the Ockham's Razor Award for Excellence in Skeptical Activism (The Skeptic Magazine and QEDcon). He has been a frequent consultant to the media on parapsychology and has made appearances on radio and television as a voice of skepticism, reasoning and science.

Stanley Krippner, Ph.D., is the Alan Watts Professor of Psychology at Saybrook University, U.S.A. He is a former president of the Parapsychological Association and has been in receipt of its lifetime career award. He is the co-editor of *Varieties of Anomalous Experience, Examining the Scientific Record*, editor of ten volumes of *Advances in Parapsychological Research*, and co-author of *Dream Telepathy*. He is a Fellow of the Society for Psychological Science and the American Psychological Association, which gave him its Award for Distinguished Contributions to the International Advancement of Psychology. He has received other awards from the Society for Clinical and Experimental Hypnosis, the Society for Psychological Hypnosis, the Society for Humanistic Psychology, and the International Association for the Study of Dreams.

Adrian Parker, Ph.D., is a clinical psychologist and qualified at the Tavistock Clinic. He was the recipient of the Perrott-Warrick Studentship in psychical research, Trinity College, Cambridge and became the first to gain a U.K. doctorate with a thesis on altered states and ESP from the University of Edinburgh. His doctoral work co-innovated the technique, known as the psi-ganzfeld, of reproducing psychic-like experiences in the laboratory. He is author of the book *States of Mind* and has over a hundred publications on altered states of consciousness and psychic experiences. He has also worked in child psychiatry and studied medical sciences before accepting a position at Gothenburg University, when a major award from the Swedish Bank Jubilee Fond (Riksbanken) enabled the development of the "Real Time Digital Ganzfeld" which is now a benchmark procedure for studying high-quality psi (psychic) events in the laboratory. Adrian is a Professor at Gothenburg University, where he is currently carrying out research into lucid dream states and exceptional experiences amongst twins, and teaches an international course on "Consciousness Studies and Psychical Research."

A BIBLIOGRAPHY FOR PSI
AND PSYCHOTHERAPY

~

This bibliography contains a list of references compiled by Dr. James Carpenter (July, 2018) specifically pertaining to psi in relation to psychotherapy. For the purpose of this book, and complementing the work of the original authors of "Psi in Psychotherapy," it is hoped that the serious reader of this book, the researchers, the counselors, psychotherapists and parapsychologists, use this list to their advantage and take their readings, research and practice far beyond the confines of this book. This is a scaled down version of the full list created by Dr. Carpenter, with those references selected for inclusion believed to be most relevant to the key themes of this book, with a few additions thrown in for good measure.

Allik, T. (2003). Psychoanalysis and the uncanny: Take two OR when disillusionment turns out to be an illusion. *Psychoanalysis and Contemporary Thought, 26*, 3-38.

Altman, N. (2007). Integrating the transpersonal with the intersubjective. *Contemporary Psychoanalysis, 43,* 526-535.

Amir, I. (2000). *Telepathic dreams in psychotherapy.* Paper presented at: Conference of the Israel Psychoanalytic Institute, 27th May.

Balint, M. (1956). Notes on parapsychology and parapsychological healing. *International Journal of Psycho-Analysis, 36*, 31-35.

Ballard, J. A. (1991). Rychlakean theory and parapsychology. *Journal of the American Society for Psychical Research, 85*, 167-181.

Bohm D (1980). *Wholeness and the implicate order.* London, U.K.: Routledge.

Bor, D. (2010). The mechanics of mind reading. *Scientific American Mind, 21,* 52-57.

Bourguignon, E. (1973). *Religion, altered states of consciousness and social change.* Columbus, OH, U.S.A.: The Ohio State University Press.

Bragdon, E. (2006). *A sourcebook for helping people with spiritual problems.* Woodstock, VT: Lightening UP Press.

Branfman, T.G., & Bunker, H.A. (1952). Three 'extra-sensory perception' dreams. *Psychoanalytic Quarterly, 21*, 190-195.

Brawar, P. A., Handal, P. J., Fabricatore, A. N., Roberts, R., & Wajda-Johnston, V. A. (2002). Training and education in religion/spirituality within APA-accredited clinical psychology programs. *Professional Psychology: Research and Practice, 33*, 203–206.

Brenninkmeijer, J. (2015). Brainwaves and psyches: A genealogy of an extended self. *History of the Human Sciences, 28*, 115-133.

Brett, C., Heriot-Maitland, C., McGuire, P., & Peters, E. (2014). Predictors of distress associated with psychotic like anomalous experiences in clinical and non-clinical populations. *British Journal of Clinical Psychology, 53*, 213-227.

Brottman, M. (2011). *Phantoms of the clinic: From thought-transference to projective identification.* London: Karnac.

Brunswick, D. (1957). A comment on E. Servadio's 'A presumptively telepathic-precognitive dream during analysis'. *International Journal of Psycho-Analysis, 38*, 56.

Cambray, J. (2011). Moments of complexity and enigmatic action: A Jungian view of the therapeutic field. *Journal of Analytical Psychology, 56*, 296-339.

Cameron, R. (2013). The energy in the room: Bodies behaving weirdly. *Psychotherapy and Politics International*, *11*, 34-39.

Campbell, J., & Pile, S. (2010). Telepathy and its vicissitudes: Freud, thought transference and the hidden lives of the (repressed and non-repressed) unconscious. *Subjectivity*, *3*, 403-425.

Cardeña, E., Lynn, S. J., & Krippner, S. (Eds.)(2014). *Varieties of anomalous experience: Examining the scientific evidence* (2nd ed.). Washington, DC, U.S.A.: American Psychological Association.

Carpenter, J.C. (1988). Parapsychology and the psychotherapy session: Their phenomenological confluence. *Journal of Parapsychology, 52*, 213-224.

Carpenter, J.C. (1988). Quasi-therapeutic group process and ESP. *Journal of Parapsychology, 52*, 279-304.

Carpenter, J.C. (2002). The intrusion of anomalous communication in group and individual psychotherapy: Clinical observations and a research project. *Proceedings of the Symposium of the Bial Foundation, 4*, 255-274.

Carpenter, J.C. (2012). *First Sight: ESP and Parapsychology in everyday life.* New York, U.S.A.: Rowman & Littlefield.

Clark, A., & Chalmers, D. (1998). The extended mind. *Annals of Internal Medicine, 58*, 7-19.

Coly, L., & McMahon, J. (Eds.) (1989). *Psi and clinical practice.* New York, U.S.A.: Parapsychology Foundation.

Cooper, C.E. (2016). The therapeutic nature of anomalous events: A union of positive psychology and parapsychology. In M.D. Smith, & P. Worth (Eds.) 2nd *Applied Positive Psychology Symposium: Proceedings of Presented Papers* (pp. 98-107). High Wycombe: Bucks New University.

Cooper, C.E., Roe, C.A., & Mitchell, G. (2015). Anomalous experiences and the bereavement process. In T. Cattoi, & C. Moreman (Eds.), *Death, dying and mysticism: The ecstasy of the end* (pp.117-131). New York: Palgrave Macmillan.

Crabtree, A. (1993). *From Mesmer to Freud: Magnetic sleep and the roots of psychological healing.* New Haven, CT, U.S.A.: Yale University Press.

Crossley, J. P., & Salter, D. P. (2005). A question of finding harmony: A grounded theory study of clinical psychologists' experience of addressing spiritual beliefs in therapy. *Psychology and Psychotherapy: Theory, Research and Practice, 78*, 295–313.

Davis, J., Lockwood, L., & Wright, C. (1991). Reasons for not reporting peak experiences. *Journal of Humanistic Psychology, 31*, 86–94.

Dein, S. (2012). Mental health and the paranormal. *International Journal of Transpersonal Studies, 3*, 61–74.

Devereux, G. (1953). *Psychoanalysis and the occult.* Madison, CT, U.S.A.: International Universities Press.

Dossey, L. (1993). *Healing words: The power of prayer and the practice of medicine.* San Francisco, U.S.A.: HarperSanFrancisco.

Ehrenwald, H.J. (1942). Telepathy in dreams. *British Journal of Medical Psychology, 19,* 313-23.

Ehrenwald, H.J. (1944). Telepathy in the psychoanalytic situation. *British Journal of Medical Psychology, 20,* 51-62.

Ehrenwald, H.J. (1950). Psychotherapy and the telepathic hypothesis. *American Journal of Psychotherapy, 4,* 51-79.

Ehrenwald, J.H. (1948). *Telepathy and medical psychology.* New York, U.S.A.: Norton.

Ehrenwald, J.H. (1950). Presumptively telepathic incidents during analysis. *Psychiatric Quarterly, 24,* 726-743.

Ehrenwald, J.H. (1955). *New dimensions in deep analysis.* New York, U.S.A.: Grune and Stratton.

Ehrenwald, J.H. (1956). Telepathy, concepts, criteria. *Psychiatric Quarterly, 30,* 425-448.

Ehrenwald, J.H. (1956). Telepathy: Concepts, criteria and consequences. *Psychiatric Quarterly, 30,* 425-444.

Ehrenwald, J.H. (1957). The telepathy hypothesis and doctrinal compliance in psychotherapy. *American Journal of Psychotherapy, 11,* 359-379.

Ehrenwald, J.H. (1960). Schizophrenia, neurotic compliance, and the psi hypothesis. *Psychoanalytic Review, 47,* 43-54.

Ehrenwald, J.H. (1970). *The ESP experience.* New York, U.S.A.: Basic Books.

Ehrenwald, J.H. (1971). Mother-child symbiosis: Cradle of ESP. *Psychoanalytic Review, 58,* 455-466.

Ehrenwald, J.H. (1972). A neurophysiological model of psi phenomenon. *Journal of Nervous and Mental Disease, 54,* 406-418.

Ehrenwald, J.H. (1977). Psi phenomena and brain research. In Benjamin Wolman (Ed.), *Handbook of parapsychology* (pp. 716-729). New York, U.S.A.: Van Nostrand Reinhold.

Eigen, M. (1998). *The psychoanalytic mystic.* New York, U.S.A.: *ESF* Publishers.

Eisenbud, J. (1946). Telepathy and the problems of psychoanalysis. *Psychoanalytic Quarterly, 15,* 32-87.

Eisenbud, J. (1946). Telepathy and problems of psychoanalysis. *Psychoanalytic Quarterly, 15,* 32-87.

Eisenbud, J. (1947). The dreams of two patients in analysis interpreted as a telepathicrève à deux. *Psychoanalytic Quarterly*,16, 39-60.

Eisenbud, J. (1948). Analysis of a presumptively telepathic dream. *Psychoanalytic Quarterly, 22,* 103-135.

Eisenbud, J. (1969). Chronologically extraordinary psi correspondences in the psychoanalytic setting. *Psychoanalytic Quarterly, 56,* 9-27.

Eisenbud, J. (1970). *Psi and psychoanalysis.* New York, U.S.A.: Grune and Stratton.

Ellenberger, H.F. (1970). *The discovery of the unconscious: The history and evolution of dynamic psychiatry.* London, U.K.: Fontana Press.

Ellis, A. (1947). Telepathy and psychoanalysis: A critique of recent 'findings'. *Psychoanalytic Quarterly, 21,* 607-659.

Ellis, A. (1949). Re-analysis of an alleged telepathic dream. *Psychoanalytic Quarterly, 23,* 116-126.

Evenden, R.E., & Cooper, C.E. (2018). Positive psychology in the clinical parapsychology setting. In M.D. Smith, & P. Worth (Eds.) *4th Applied Positive Psychology Symposium: Proceedings of Presented Papers* (pp.192-203).High Wycombe: Bucks New University.

Evrard, R., Massicotte, C., & Rabeyron, T. (2017). *Freud as a psychical researcher: The impossible Freudian legacy*. Presented at Sixtieth Annual Convention of the Parapsychological Association, 23rd July.

Farber, S.K. (2017). Becoming a telepathic tuning fork: Anomalous experience and the relational mind. *Psychoanalytic Dialogues, 27,* 719-734.

Farrell, D. (1983). Freud's 'thought-transference', repression, and the future of psychoanalysis. *International Journal of Psycho-Analysis, 64,* 71-81.

Fodor, N. (1947). Telepathy in analysis: A discussion of five dreams. *Psychoanalytic Quarterly, 21,* 171-189.

Gay, P. (1988). *Freud: A life for our time.* New York, U.S.A.: W.W. Norton.

Georgescu, M. (2013). The feeling of the uncanny, cruelty and the principles of synchronicity - a case study based on multiple coincidences. *Procedia: Social and Behavioural Sciences, 78,* 26-30.

Greyson, B. (1977). Telepathy in mental illness: Deluge or delusion? *Journal of Nervous and Mental Disease, 165,* 184-200.

Grof, S., & Grof, C. (Eds.)(1989). *Spiritual emergency: When personal transformation becomes a crisis.* Los Angeles, CA, U.S.A.: J. P. Tarcher.

Gustafson, A. (1966). I use ESP in psychotherapy. *Fate, 19* (11), 86-93.

Hall, J.A. (1988). Jungian analytic meaning of clinical parapsychological phenomena. *ASPR Newsletter, 14*, 9-11.

Hastings, A. (1983). A counseling approach to parapsychological experience. *Journal of Transpersonal Psychology, 15*, 143– 167.

Hewitt, M.A. (2014). Freud and the psychoanalysis of telepathy: Commentary on Claudie Massicotte's "Psychical transmissions." *Psychoanalytic Dialogues: International Journal of Relational Perspectives, 24*, 103-108.

Hitschmann, E. (1924). Telepathy and psycho-analysis. *International Journal of Psycho-Analysis, 5*, 425-439.

Jafari, S. (2016). Religion and spirituality within counseling/clinical psychology training programmes: A systematic review. *British Journal of Guidance and Counseling, 44*, 257–267.

Kennedy, J. E., & Kanthamani, H. (1995). An exploratory study of the effects of paranormal and spiritual experiences on people's lives and well-being. *Journal of the American Society for Psychical Research, 89*, 249–264.

Knox, S., Catlin, L. A., Casper, M., & Schlosser, L. Z. (2005). Addressing religion and spirituality in psychotherapy: Clients' perspectives. *Psychotherapy Research, 15*, 287–303.

Kramer, W., Bauer, E., & Hövelmann, G. (Eds.)(2012). *Perspectives of clinical parapsychology: An introductory reader.* Bunnik, Netherlands: Stichting Het Johan Borgman Fonds.

Krippner, S., & Friedman, H. L. (2010). *Debating psychic experience: Human potential or human illusion?* New York, U.S.A.: Praeger.

Lazar, S.G. (2001). Knowing, influencing, and healing: Paranormal phenomena and implications for psychoanalysis and psychotherapy. *Psychoanalytic Inquiry, 21,* 113-31.

LeShan, L. (1991). The many roads to becoming a psychic healer: A research approach and personal adventure. *ASPR Newsletter, 17* (2), 25-29.

Lucas, C. G. (2011). *In case of spiritual emergency: Moving successfully through your awakening.* Forres, Scotland, U.K.: Findhorn Press.

Major, R. & Miller, P. (1981). Empathy, antipathy and telepathy in the analytic process. *Psychoanalytic Inquiry, 1,* 449-470.

Marlo, H., & Kline, J.S. (1998). Synchronicity and psychotherapy: Unconscious communication in the psychotherapeutic relationship. *Psychotherapy, 35,* 13-22.

Massicotte, C. (2014). Psychical transmissions: Freud, spiritualism, and the occult. *Psychoanalytic Dialogues. 24,* 88-102.

Mayer, E.L. (2001). On "telepathic dreams?": An unpublished paper by Robert J. Stoller. *Journal of the American Psychoanalytic Association, 49*, 629-657.

Mayer, E.L. (2007*). Extraordinary knowing: Science, skepticism, and the inexplicable powers of the human mind.* New York, U.S.A.: Bantam,

Mintz, E.E. with Schmeidler, G. (1983). *The psychic thread: Paranormal and transpersonal aspects of psychotherapy.* New York, U.S.A.: Human Science Press.

Moreira-Almeida, A., Koenig, H. G., & Lucchetti, G. (2014). Clinical implications of spirituality to mental health: Review of evidence and practical guidelines. *Revista Brasileira Psiquiatria, 36*, 176–182.

Murray, C. (Ed.) (2012). *Mental health and anomalous experiences.* New York, U.S.A.: Nova Science Publishers.

Nelson, M.C. (1965). Birds of a feather: Psychoanalytyic observations on parapsychological phenomena. *Israeli Annals of Psychiatry & Related Disciplines, 3*, 73-87.

Nelson, M.C. (1975). Psi in the family. *Clinical Social Work Journal, 3*, 279-285.

Nelson, M.C. (1988). Imagery, self-containment and psi. *Psychotherapy Patient, 4*, 345-360.

Pechey, R., & Halligan, P. (2012). Prevalence and correlates of anomalous experiences in a large nonclinical sample. *Psychology and Psychotherapy: Theory, Research and Practice, 85,* 150–162.

Pederson-Krag, G. (1947). Telepathy and repression. *Psychoanalytic Quarterly, 16,* 61-68.

Rabeyron, T., & Watt, C. (2010). Paranormal experiences, mental health and mental boundaries, and psi. *Personality and Individual Differences, 48,* 487–492.

Reik, T. (1948). *Listening with the third ear.* New York, U.S.A.: Farrar, Strauss and Giroux.

Rieff, P. (Ed.)(1963). *Freud: Studies in parapsychology.* New York, U.S.A.: Collier Books.

Ringstrom, P. (2001). Cultivating the improvisational in psychoanalytic treatment. *Psychoanalytic Dialogues, 11,* 754.

Roheim, G. (1932). Telepathy in a dream. *Psychoanalytic Quarterly, 1,* 277-291.

Rosenbaum, R. (2011). Exploring the other dark continent: Parallels between psi phenomena and the psychotherapeutic process. *Psychoanalytic Review, 98,* 57-90.

Roudinesco E. (2001). *Why psychoanalysis?* [R. Bowlby translator]. New York, U.S.A.: Columbia.

Roxburgh, E. C., & Evenden, R. E. (2016). 'They daren't tell people': Therapists experiences of working with clients who report anomalous experiences [Special Issue]. *European Journal of Psychotherapy and Counseling, 18*, 123–141.

Roxburgh, E. C., & Evenden, R. E. (2016). It's about having exposure to this: Investigating the training needs of therapists in relation to the issue of anomalous experiences. *British Journal of Guidance & Counseling, 44*, 540-549.

Roxburgh, E. C., & Evenden, R. E. (2016). Most people think you're a fruit loop: Clients' experiences of seeking support for anomalous experiences. *Counseling and Psychotherapy Research 16*, 211-221.

Roxburgh, E. C., & Roe, C. A. (2011). A survey of dissociation, boundary-thinness and psychological wellbeing in Spiritualist mental mediumship. *Journal of Parapsychology, 75*, 279–299.

Roxburgh, E. C., & Roe, C. A. (2014). Reframing voices and visions using a spiritual model: An interpretative phenomenological analysis of anomalous experiences in mediumship. *Mental Health, Religion, & Culture, 17*, 641–653.

Roxburgh, E. C., Ridgway, S., & Roe, C. (2015). Exploring the meaning in meaningful coincidences: An interpretative phenomenological analysis of synchronicity in therapy [Special Issue]. *European Journal of Psychotherapy and Counseling, 17*, 144–161.

Roxburgh, E. C., Ridgway, S., & Roe, C. A. (2016). Synchronicity in the therapeutic setting: A survey of practitioners. *Counseling and Psychotherapy Research, 16,* 44–53.

Schmeidler, G.R. (Ed.)(1976). *Parapsychology: Its relationship to physics, biology, psychology, and psychiatry.* Metuchen, NJ, U.S.A.: Scarecrow Press.

Schwarz, B.E. (1969). Synchronicity and telepathy. *Psychoanalytic Review, 56,* 44-56.

Servadio, E. (1955). A presumptively telepathic-precognitive dream during analysis. *International Journal of Psycho-Analysis, 36,* 27-30.

Servadio, E. (1956). Transference and thought-transference. *International Journal of Psycho-Analysis, 37,* 392-95.

Shainberg, D. (1976). Telepathy in psychoanalysis: An instance. *American Journal Psychotherapy, 30,* 463-472.

Siegel, C. (1986). Parapsychological counseling: Six patterns of response to spontaneous psychic experiences. In W. G. Roll (Ed.), *Research in parapsychology* (pp.172–174). Metuchen, NJ, U.S.A.: Scarecrow Press.

Simmonds-Moore, C. (Ed.) (2012). *Exceptional experience and health: Essays on mind, body and human potential.* Jefferson, NC, U.S.A.: McFarland.

Steffen, E., Wilde, D., & Cooper, C.E. (2017). Affirming the positive in anomalous experiences: A challenge to dominant accounts of reality, life and death. In N. J.L. Brown, T. Lomas, & F.J. Eiroá (Eds.), *International Handbook of Critical Positive Psychology: A Synthesis for Social Change* (pp.227-244). London, U.K.: Routledge.

Stolorow, R. (1991). The intersubjective context of intrapsychic experience: A decade of psychoanalytic inquiry. *Psychoanalytic Inquiry, 11,* 171-184.

Strean, H.S., & Coleman-Nelson, M. (1962). A further clinical illustration of the paranormal triangle hypothesis. *Psychoanalysis and the Psychoanalytic Review, 49,* 61-76.

Symington, N. (1998). *Emotion and spirit: Questioning the claims of psychoanalysis and religion.* London, U.K.: Karnac.

Taylor, S. F. (2005). Between the idea and the reality: A study of the counseling experiences of bereaved people who sense the presence of the deceased. *Counseling and Psychotherapy Research, 5,* 53-61.

Tennes, M. (2007). Beyond intersubjectivity: The transpersonal dimension of the psychoanalytic encounter. *Contemporary Psychoanalysis, 43,* 505-525.

Totten, N. (Ed.)(2003). *Psychoanalysis and the paranormal: Lands of darkness.* London, U.K.: Karnac.

Totton, N. (2007). "Funny you should say that": paranormality, at the margins and the centre of psychotherapy. *European Journal of Psychotherapy and Counseling, 9,* 389-401.

Ullman, M. (1975). Parapsychology and psychiatry. In A.M. Freeman, H. I. Kaplan, and B. J. Saddock (Eds.), *Comprehensive Textbook of Psychiatry, 2*nd *ed.,* Vol. 2 (pp. 2552-2561). Baltimore, U.S.A.: Williams and Wilkins.

Weiler, R.B. (1967). Apparent telepathy in psychotherapy. *Psychiatric Quarterly, 41,* 448-473.

Wilde, D. J., & Murray, C. D. (2009). The evolving self: Finding meaning in near-death experiences using interpretative phenomenological analysis. *Mental Health, Religion and Culture, 12,* 223–239.

Williams, M. (1963). The Poltergeist Man. *Journal of Analytical Psychology, 8,* 123-144.

Wilner, W. (1996). Dreams and the holistic nature of interpersonal psychoanalytic experience. *Psychoanalytic Dialogues: International Journal of Relational Perspectives, 6,* 813-830.

Wooffitt, R. (2016). Relational psychoanalysis and anomalous communication: Continuities and discontinuities in psychoanalysis and telepathy. *History of the Human Sciences, 30,* 118-137.

Zorab, G. (1957). ESP experiments with psychotics. *Journal of the American Society for Psychical Research, 39,* 162-164.

INDEX

~

F

G

www.ingramcontent.com/pod-product-compliance
Lightning Source LLC
Chambersburg PA
CBHW022127080426

42734CB00006B/257